Wilt Thou Be Made Whole?

Healing Life's Hurts

Drs. David and Vernette Rosier

Treasure House

An Imprint of

Destiny Image₊ Publishers, Inc.
P.O. Box 310
Shippensburg, PA 17257-0310

"For where your treasure is
there will your heart be also." Matthew 6:21

ISBN 1-56043-267-5

For Worldwide Distribution
Printed in the U.S.A.

Treasure House books are available through these fine distributors outside the United States:

Christian Growth, Inc.
Jalan Kilang-Timor, Singapore 0315

Vine Christian Centre
Mid Glamorgan, Wales, United Kingdom

Rhema Ministries Trading
Randburg, South Africa

Omega Distributors
Ponsonby, Auckland, New Zealand

Salvation Book Centre
Petaling, Jaya, Malaysia

WA Buchanan Company
Geebung, Queensland, Australia

Successful Christian Living
Capetown, Rep. of South Africa

Word Alive
Niverville, Manitoba, Canada

Inside the U.S., call toll free to order:
1-800-722-6774
Or reach us on the Internet:
http://www.reapernet.com

Dedication

To our children Jerrod, Byron, Daveron, and Marcus: Special thanks for working so harmoniously with us. Without your cooperation we couldn't have completed this book.

To Sheri Byas, Rosalyn Best, Charlotte Blue, and Cynthia Stanley: Thanks a million for the endless hours of transcribing and typing.

Thank you, Fellowship Church of Praise, for your prayers and support.

Special thanks to Evangelist Diane Smith for her expertise and invaluable ideas that helped us articulate our thoughts. To Pastor Cherry Simmons for endless hours of editing. Our deepest appreciation to Pastor Claudia Brown for her research and Introduction.

Contents

Foreword vii

Introduction. ix

Chapter 1 Turn Your Wounds to Scars 1

Chapter 2 Frustration 15

Chapter 3 Facing Adversity and
Healing Life's Hurts 29

Chapter 4 Dealing With Offenses and Failure 45

Chapter 5 Make Me Whole! 63

Chapter 6 God Mixes the Bitter With the Sweet . . . 75

Chapter 7 You Can Make It 93

A Brief History of the Panama City
Fellowship Church of Praise. 109

Foreword

It is truly an honor for Pastors David and Vernette Rosier to ask me to write the Foreword to their new book, *Wilt Thou Be Made Whole?* I have admired their work for several years and have been personally helped through their teaching.

I know them to be mightily used by God, yet to be so down to earth. They teach where we all live. There are real hurts and wounds in the world as well as in the Body of Christ, but most of us only deal with them at special occasions like a women's meeting or at a men's retreat. Hurts and wounds happen to all of us on a daily basis and we don't have the faintest idea how to deal with them. We as pastors and leaders must learn how to "turn these wounds into scars."

If you don't deal with your past, your past will deal with you! People have experienced firsthand the devastating results of not dealing with their past.

Within the Rosiers' local body, it is a constant practice to expose and deal with hurts and wounds. I have listened to their teachings and used them in my own meetings. I know you will be thoroughly blessed as you journey through the wealth of information that has been carefully and prayerfully put together to help "make you whole."

Pastor Candi Staton Sussewell
Co-Pastor of Upon This Rock Family Church
Decatur, Georgia

Introduction

Thou art worthy, O Lord, to receive glory and honour and power: for Thou hast created all things, and for Thy pleasure they are and were created (Revelation 4:11).

Each of us was born with a purpose. Jesus Christ is telling us, "I want you to do the will of My Father—regardless of past hurts, pressures, and failures." We have all encountered pain or difficulty as children or teenagers, but these things shouldn't stop us from being what God wants us to be.

The good news proclaimed in this book is that God is greater than anything we have ever experienced. God wants our hurts and failures to become stepping-stones, not hindrances.

In the natural, you may have come from a dysfunctional family, but you belong to a new family now. The Body of Christ, the Church, *is not a broken home!* We cannot continue to complain about the wrongs suffered 20 years ago—it's time for us to deal with them and move on. This book will help you deal with hidden hindrances that may be hampering your success. Expect God to transform, heal, deliver, and set you free as you move through these anointed pages.

As a counselor at a treatment center for alcoholics, drug addicts, and other life dysfunctions, I've noticed that most of our clients experienced severe trauma as children. Many come from broken homes, and were rejected or molested by a parent or some other trusted member of the family. Many of these people rotate through "the system" repeatedly because they have never identified or acknowledged the source or root of their problems.

Secular psychologists, counselors, and psychiatrists will probe and question hurting people to help them vent their frustrations, relieve pressure, and share their needs. Unfortunately, they often fail to discover the root of a problem due to the suppression, the tendency *"to press down, to hide, to act as if it didn't happen."* When they do find the problem, they are generally helpless to deal with it apart from the power of the Holy Spirit.

If you want to kill a tree, you'd better dig through the soil and get to the root. Cutting off the branches and the leaves won't do it. Many of us have picked leaves off and cut off branches, but we have not reached the root. God is waiting for us to yield to Him so He can dig through the soil, expose the root, and deal with it once and for all.

As Christians, we have the anointing, we have the Holy Spirit, we have pastors, and we have a whole family of brothers and sisters in Christ. Although we will face problems, we should not be struggling like the world struggles. We need to get healed and go out and tell the world: "Hey listen, you've been going to therapy for 40 years and you still can't get it together. Let me tell you about a Healer…"

God wants to restore us to wholeness. He sees the potential in you and me. He knows what we can do because He made us. This book by Drs. David and Vernette Rosier echoes the words of Jesus to the crippled man beside the pool of Bethesda, "Wilt thou be made whole?" No matter what we have experienced in our past, our future begins with our answer to this question.

Pastor Claudia Brown
Chemical Addictions Therapist
Tuskegee, Alabama

Chapter 1

Turn Your Wounds to Scars

If you are breathing, then you have been wounded. Wounds come naturally in the battle of life, and as Christians, we should know that wounds are an unavoidable risk we face as soldiers of the light. We are convinced that most believers have been looking at wounds in the wrong way: God wants us to shake off some harmful preconceptions about hurts, wounds, and scars. Sure we've been wounded, but *God has made provision for our healing* from every battle wound! He is determined to set us free from shame, rejection, and the hurts of the past—*if we let Him*! He is trying to teach us how to "turn our wounds to scars of victory"!

A wound is "an injury to the body (as from violence, accident, or surgery) that involves laceration or breaking of a membrane (as the skin) and usually damage to the underlying tissues," and "a mental or emotional hurt or blow."[1] The way we treat our wounds determines whether they heal, fester, or produce death. When wounds are ignored or allowed to fester, *gangrene* often sets in. Gangrene comes from a Greek word that means "to gnaw." It refers to the "local death of soft tissues due to loss of blood supply" and "pervasive decay or corruption."[2]

Scars: The Seal of Survival

Do you know how gangrene is treated? Since it always involves the death of tissues and represents a vital danger to the living tissues nearby, doctors usually amputate the affected part to preserve the life of the victim! God's ideal provision is for our wounds to be exposed, treated, and allowed to heal, leaving only the scars behind as the seal of our survival and the proof that we have overcome. Gangrene is a product of neglect or the avoidance of proper treatment.

When we are wounded, the nerves around the wound are extra sensitive to irritation or pain. Sometimes our minds are raw, like nerve endings. If you discover that every time someone comes near, you think, "They're probably thinking something negative," then that is a sign that your mind has not been healed. The hurt is still alive, flowing and pulsating in that wound because you've not allowed the blood of Jesus to rush in and bring healing.

Anytime an infection arises in a wound or injury to the physical body, blood rushes to that particular spot and promotes healing! At the point where you've been wounded in your spirit and emotions, all the blood shed by Jesus rushes to that spot to promote healing! Unforgiveness prevents the blood of Jesus from bringing healing to that wounded area. If we refuse to forgive those who hurt us, then we are blocking the healing blood flow to our wounds. We are setting ourselves up for the onset of gangrene! The blood is trying to rush in there but we've put a tourniquet on it; we've cut off the life-giving flow of the blood of Jesus!

God's will is for our scars to actually become our "credentials," convincing evidence that we are qualified to help others through their battles and struggles. Battle-proven soldiers with plenty of scars make the best drill sergeants in military boot camps—they've survived the dangers of battle, and they mercilessly prepare their young recruits so they too will survive in real battle. Nearly every genuine believer looks forward to seeing the "scars in the hands of Jesus" when we meet Him face to face. Why? Those scars are an incredible testimony to His great love and sacrifice for us!

Has anyone ever told you, "It's easy for you to talk because you've never been through what I've been through! You don't know what it's like"? When you've got the scars, you can say, "Not so fast—I've been through it, but I am healed; and I'm not bound by it any longer!"

Bitterness in the Barrel

"What does this have to do with me?" you ask. "What does it have to do with my church?" It has *everything* to do with you and your church! The church is made up of real people, and most of them have real hurts and wounds received in their childhood or even in the Sunday morning service! When a person is still wounded, the infection in their open wound is still oozing out. The poison of bitterness oozing from a wounded spirit can easily begin to work in the hearts around it, like one decaying apple hidden at the bottom of an apple barrel. Frankly, a wounded person who has not received God's "treatment" or provision is a dangerous person. Bitter people can't help but spew their bitterness into the lives of everyone around them!

We fail to receive God's treatment for a lot of reasons—some out of ignorance; others out of obstinacy. God's Word and books like this one can help remove the ignorance, but only we can remove the obstinacy!

The human body can cover all but the most serious wounds with a protective fluid that turns into a "scab" as the wounds heal. But this outward "covering" may sometimes conceal something very deadly, especially where the wounds are deep (as in a gunshot or stab wound), or extensive (as in a severe burn).

Vernette: Healed From the Inside Out

When I was ten years old, I accidentally shot myself in the leg with a .32 caliber pistol. A prisoner had escaped from a jail near our house, and I was taking the gun to my grandmother who was in another room. I was trying so hard to point the gun toward the ground that I bumped against a door and the gun went off! I thought I had shot a hole in the wall of the house, but when I looked down, my whole leg was red. I screamed, "Oh God, I shot my leg off!" (The doctor told me that I had barely missed the bone by just a fraction of an inch.)

That doctor treated my leg and sent me home with orders to return after a scab had formed over my wound. Every time I went back to the doctor, he would *pull off that scab* and run a cotton swab through that hole several times! I thought to my-self, *What kind of doctor is this? If he would just leave it alone, it would be healed by now.* I thank God He was really looking after me. He made sure that doctor had the training and wisdom to know that *that scab was hiding a place that could become infected*!

Every time I visited the doctor, he would remove the scab and clean the wound, saying, "I want you to heal *from the inside out.*" Even though the wound had stopped bleeding and oozing, and even though I thought it was healed, there was a hidden infection that had to be removed if I was to really heal and recover.

Is There a Doctor in Your House?

Sometimes we are like that gunshot wound. We have gone through terrible emotional hurts, rejection, or be-trayal. We come to church wearing a little scab on the outside that gives the appearance of being healed. Fortu-nately, God sends "spiritual doctors" to us who have su-pernatural discernment, compassion, and wisdom to deal with these inner wounds and bring deliverance. They can tell when the "scabs" are hiding emotional or spiritual in-fection, and they'll pull it off—even when we scream and protest. Since this treatment process can be painful, most of us try to avoid "doctors" and treatments!

The truth is that many times the things we use to cover up our wounds actually cover a deadly poison of bit-terness, and prevent our healing! The question Jesus asks all of us who have wounds is the same question He asked the lame man at the pool of Bethesda centuries ago: "Wilt thou be made whole?" (Jn. 5:6)

Look at My Scars!

The scars of Jesus give us a divine pattern for healing the wounds in our lives. They are an eternal proof of supernatural recovery that destroys unbelief in those who will receive it. There is also another pattern that most of us follow at one time or another. Many Christians today, especially hurting and wounded believers, when told that they can recover from their wounds, echo the cynical words of Thomas, the "doubting disciple" of Jesus. This man was deeply disappointed and wounded when his beloved Savior died and His body mysteriously disappeared from the tomb. He was afraid to believe in a miracle. When the other disciples told him that Jesus had risen from the dead and appeared to them, Thomas retreated in his pain and bitterness and bluntly told them:

...Except I shall see in His hands the print of the nails, and put my finger into the print of the nails, and thrust my hand into His side, I will not believe (John 20:25).

Eight days later, Thomas reaped what he had sown. The Gospel of John says the disciples had gathered together again, but this time, Thomas made it to the meeting. Suddenly Jesus came into the locked room, even though the doors were shut. As He stood in the middle of the group, Jesus calmed them down. Then He turned to Thomas and said:

...Reach hither thy finger, and behold My hands; and reach hither thy hand, and thrust it into My side: and be not faithless, but believing. And

Thomas answered and said unto Him, My Lord and my God (John 20:27-28).

Thomas literally was able to thrust his hand into the deep scar in Jesus' side, and to touch the large nail scars or "prints" in the Lord's hands! The Lord was demonstrating that even though He had been wounded unto death, His scars were absolute proof of His identity and complete healing. Perhaps it isn't an "accident" that the Greek word *tupos*, translated here as "print," literally means "the mark of a stroke or blow...an example, *the pattern.*"[3]

The Pattern for Healing

The prints or nail scars of Jesus removed the doubts of Thomas and established a "pattern" for our own healing. In the same way, the scars from hurtful wounds you have survived in your own life will quell doubts in the minds of people who ask you, "How could you go through that experience? How could you be so betrayed and hurt by someone in the church, and still walk in love and be healed?"

What is God's goal in this healing process? He wants us to be released to heal others! Jesus rose from the grave to raise others. He wants us to do the same thing with every hurt or wound we encounter. Each time someone asks about your limp or your scar, *if you have really gone all the way through the healing process*, then you can tell them, "Beloved, I got through it by the grace of God, and I have total victory! Let me tell you how you can come through your pain too! I know you are wounded, but you can be completely healed—and don't tell me you can't! If I can make it through, you can too. I'm a living testimony that even if you've been wounded and injured in the 'House of God'—you can walk in triumph and wholeness!"

Let Me See Your Scars!

Believers and unbelievers alike are challenging believers in the Church, "Let me see your scars, and then I'll believe your testimony. I want proof of your healing God! Show me your scars and I'll believe that you have been through hard places and that you've got the victory. Prove to me that even though you're still going through things, you're not bitter." Unfortunately, many of us are walking around with infected, oozing, unhealed wounds, and the world says, "Hey, you're still in the same shape I'm in! Why should I believe your God offers something better?"

Don't be upset at unbelievers or even at other Christians who say, "Show me your scars." They're just looking for a print or a pattern they can follow and trust! They are hurting people, and they are demanding proof that we've risen above our wounds before they trust our counsel or receive our love. That's what Thomas was saying to Jesus: "If that's *really* You, Jesus, then You will show me the scars. I know You were pierced in the side. I know that they put nails in Your hands and feet." When Jesus told Thomas to put his hands right into those old wounds, it proved something that is very important to us today: If Jesus had still been *sensitive* in those areas, He wouldn't have been able to *bear the pain* when Thomas touched the nail prints!

People who are still wounded desperately fear being hurt again. They surround themselves with a "self-space" that you can't penetrate without God's help. Whenever you approach them in friendship, they will often back up and say, "No, the last time I had friends, they wounded me."

Can You Love Your Betrayer?

In our ministry, we have experienced personal betrayals and painful wounds. People have asked us, "How in the world can you love and be friends with the very person who tried to ruin your reputation? He tried to destroy your ministry! He tried to cause trouble in your marriage! How can you love the one who betrayed you?"

The answer doesn't point to us—we have a divine "Pattern." We are commissioned by God to treat our "Judas" friends the same way Jesus treated His—with love (see Mt. 26:21-24; Lk. 22:3). God is telling each of us, "Beloved, I don't want you to stay wounded the rest of your days. You are spewing that bitterness on everyone you meet. You're not just poisoning your own life—the effects of your wounds are running through your *bloodline*. This can cause your children to be filled with bitterness as you sow it into their lives through your words!"

Have you ever seen a parent who was wounded by friends hold his child up close to him and say, *"Baby, you don't need any friends. I remember when I had friends, and I don't want you hurt. Come on and stick with me."* That's sowing bitterness into their *spiritual* bloodstream. Those words are *wounding* those little children because they amount to curses! Those evil words of bitterness, disguised as words of protection, will actually hinder those children by transferring the parent's phobia (or fear) to the child!

The Walls That Bind

Unforgiveness and bitterness act as walls around our hearts and souls. China's civilization was so far ahead of the surrounding countries that China's rulers decided to build a great wall so no one could see what they had and plunder the country. Hundreds of years later, the walls were finally breached, but by then other civilizations had advanced far beyond the isolated Chinese world and left them far behind!

When you build walls to keep people out, you also put one person in a cage: yourself. You are *bound* by the very "protection" you created for yourself. As long as those unnatural walls remain, you cannot receive healing. Bitterness and unforgiveness raise up walls that love's healing can't get through. Those walls don't really protect you—they hinder and imprison you!

It has been proven that people can "will to die." Scientists have shown that you don't have to be physically sick. You can decide that you're tired of living, and die. The human mind is incredibly powerful because God made it that way. Many times, when a person's lifelong spouse dies, the surviving spouse will die soon after, even though they had no health problems or physical causes for their death. In the same way, if you decide that you want to be *healed* of the wounds and injuries that have traumatized your life, you can and will be healed!

Get Them, God!

In the midst of His wounds, with the nails in His hands, nails in His feet, and agonizing on that cross, Jesus looked down—not after He was healed—but in the midst of the bleeding, in the midst of the pain, the suffering, and the affliction, and He said, "Forgive them!" Yet many of us refuse to carry our cross of afflictions. He has shown us the way to forgiveness and healing, but we are still saying, "Don't forgive them! Get them, God!"

If you are being "nailed to the cross" by cruel treatment, if you're being crucified by gossip or slander, remember that Jesus promised never to leave or forsake you (see Heb. 13:5)! Your response will determine if you're willing to "die to self"—self-interest, self-defense, and self-protection. If you die to self, you will bring life to others around you. It happens when you choose to love and forgive others—even when they mistreat you.

Old soldiers have many scars, but the scars are proof of the great battles they have survived and won in the spiritual realm. If there are no scars, it probably means there were no battles endured or victories won. Wounds don't simply show how many times you've "let the enemy defeat you." They are a record of how many times you have *survived, risen, and stood up after a fall or hard hit*! Are you still sulking and nursing an old dried-out scab in that same spot where you were "stabbed" by a friend ten years ago? Get up and go forward!

Don't Stay on the Cross!

Jesus didn't remain on that cross. He rose to demonstrate His total victory and power over death, hell, and all of hell's plans to wound and destroy lives. When the Word of God says, "By His stripes we are healed" (see 1 Pet. 2:24), it means He took our hurts and wounds and dealt with them. When they offered Him a bitter drink on the cross, He showed us that we're going to have bitter situations. Bitter circumstances will come into our lives, but we don't have to receive them. He refused them. You don't have to take in bitterness. What we *can* do is understand who is in authority, and who has all power. If we stand in the authority of His Name and refuse to receive the bitterness and unforgiveness—then we will see the enemy routed and walk in wholeness.

How Will You Respond?

What are you going to do with the bitterness that has plagued your life? If you're brought face-to-face with it again, how will you respond? Sometimes there are badly wounded areas in our lives that we claim are healed, but they are still super-sensitive. When someone's words or certain situations touch those sensitive places, we react violently. Jesus will allow circumstances to touch those hidden sore spots to show us that we are still hurting.

When we discover that we still have pain, we may realize that it's time we allow God to heal and "desensitize" those injured places. It's time to let God remove the scab that hinders our healing. We must trust the Great Physician to go beyond our frustration, our protests, and our outward disguises to open our hidden wounds and purge away the infection of bitterness, judgment, and hurt!

Healing begins on the inside. Our Great Physician knows what to look for. He knows whether our wounds are really healing on the inside, or if a "scab" of religiosity, pride, or fear has sealed in the infection and is preventing complete recovery! Allow the Lord to remove the spiritual scabs that prevent you from healing. As you forgive and release judgment and bitterness, you too will experience complete recovery! Only the Balm of Gilead will turn your scabs into glorious scars of victory and emblems of God's faithfulness in the fire!

End Notes

1. Merriam Webster's Collegiate Dictionary, 10th Edition (Springfield, MA, 1994), pp. 1365-1366.

2. Merriam Webster's Collegiate Dictionary, p. 479.

3. *Strong's Concordance* (James Strong, *The Exhaustive Concordance of the Bible*, Peabody, MA: Hendrickson Publishers, n.d.), excerpts from definition #5179 (Greek).

Chapter 2

Frustration

David was a man who knew how to worship God. He was known as a "praiser." David had learned how to keep joy stirred up in his life, but one day he came face to face with a terrible situation! He was already running for his life from his own king and living the life of an outlaw. Now his enemies had sent so much against him that he got *frustrated*. In fact, he was so frustrated that, for awhile, he completely forgot his game plan! Have you ever been in that kind of tight spot?

David had been caught completely off guard. While he and his men were away from their home in exile (Ziklag, in southern Philistia), the Amalekites invaded south Philistia! What David's band found when they came home broke their hearts.

So David and his men came to the city, and, behold, it was burned with fire; and their wives, and their sons, and their daughters, were taken captives. Then David and the people that were with him lifted up their voice and wept, until they had no more power to weep (1 Samuel 30:3-4).

David came home looking for a warm welcome, but his family was gone! They had been taken captive by one of the cruelest nations of that time! David was *frustrated*!

There are many frustrated people in the Church today! They have been hurt and the bitterness that is brewing in them could poison the lives and emotions of the next generation! All of us have to learn to keep bitterness out and keep joy flowing in our lives. Frustration and bitterness are in opposition to joy. Nehemiah the prophet knew about frustration. He fought against political systems and bitter enemies to rebuild the walls of Jerusalem and restore the faith of Israel. In the face of impossibility, he declared, "…the joy of the Lord is your strength" (Neh. 8:10). The Hebrew word translated as "strength" in this verse means "a fortified place…a defense."[1]

Frustration Makes You Lose

When we get frustrated we become ineffective. In competitive sports like boxing or tennis, you can win easily if you ever get your opponents frustrated, for they will lose their game plan. We have lost our "game plan" too often in the Church because of frustration. When we say, "Lift up your hands in joy to the Lord and glorify Him! You will see Him working in your situation," many of us lift our hands, but not all of us mix our obedience with *faith*. Sometimes we just lift our hands "because everyone else is doing it." Meanwhile, we are so frustrated that we can't feel an "ounce" of excitement, joy, or faith—even with our hands raised. Some of us will even admit to feeling resentful toward the people beside us who dare to be excited while we feel so bad!

Sometimes Christians go through so much pain and frustration that they just don't believe anything will work any more. They get their eyes on their terrible circumstances when they *should* be keeping their eyes and attention on Jesus. Frustration always comes to bless those who meditate on their circumstances, and it will cause them to be ineffective and defeated.

Frustration means "to make ineffectual: bring to nothing...impede, obstruct...to make invalid or of no effect. ... [To] *frustrate* implies making vain or ineffectual all efforts however vigorous or persistent."[2] The enemy wants us to think that our prayers and our praise are ineffective. He wants us to think we are "just going through the motions with no expectation of anything taking place in our hearts or lives." When we reach this stage, we are not releasing our faith.

You Can't Hide What's Inside

Many marriages today are marked by terrible frustration because husbands and wives have failed to deal with problems from their past. Anything we are unwilling or unable to deal with will eventually come to the surface! If they are still ignored, then our children will be affected by the same things. If we are always irritated and say unkind and critical things to our spouses, our children will hear. *It is hard to hide what is inside!* Jesus said, "...out of the abundance of the heart the mouth speaketh" (Mt. 12:34).

How do you respond when you are in your Ziklag? How do you act when you receive a bad report after everything else has already gone wrong? You have testified to others about God's care for you, and yet horrible things are happening to you! Can you still praise Him?

Don't be surprised or caught off guard by the devil—he is always trying to send you some kind of bad news, hoping to get you frustrated. Do you remember Job's story? Every time the devil attacked, he always left one person to go back and tell Job all the bad news. The devil always sends somebody to tell you all the bad things others say about you. Do you have a "nagger" in your life like Job's wife? (No, we're not necessarily talking about your spouse!) You probably have a good supply of "Job's comforters" just waiting to give you "their two-cents' worth" about your problems, along with the latest things "they" are saying about you.

Love Your "Judas"

You may not realize it, but you also have a "Judas" in your life! We believe we are supposed to have one—everybody needs a Judas. Don't get frustrated by what you just read! Think about this: A "Judas" is a person who acts friendly, who pretends to love you and stand by you, but who in reality is stabbing you in the back. Do you realize that your "Judas" is helping you to draw closer to God? It's true! Jesus needed Judas—He couldn't have fulfilled His divine mission of atonement without him! We need a Judas too. (Don't try to figure out who it is; you will just damage someone who truly is your friend.)

David was frustrated that day as he stood in the smoky remains of his home, with his ears filled with the angry, heartbroken cries of his men. David the mighty warrior cried until he could cry no more. The Bible says,

"And David's two wives were taken captives, Ahinoam the Jezreelitess, and Abigail the wife of Nabal the Carmelite" (1 Sam. 30:5). Then David's bad situation suddenly got worse: "And David was greatly distressed; *for the people spake of stoning him...*" (1 Sam. 30:6).

When the Bible says David was "greatly distressed," it means he was literally suffering physical and mental pain. The crushing weight of his circumstances hurt his heart. At that point, David could have said, "Here I am, out doing the work of God, and I've lost all that is important to me!" Fortunately, David knew he couldn't afford to stay frustrated, or he wouldn't achieve his divine destiny.

Why Should I Pray?

He must have thought to himself, *If I get to the point where I forget what I'm supposed to do, I won't make it!* Have you ever been so frustrated that you said, "Why should I pray?" If you begin to complain and let your frustration take over, you will stop seeking God, and then you *will* be in a hopeless situation.

David had not only lost his wives, his family, and his possessions, but now his "church members" had turned into an angry mob and were talking about stoning him! "If we weren't in your church, David, this wouldn't have happened to us! We should have stayed where we were. We came over here to your church, and now look what has happened to us! People are talking about us, and now we've lost everything! We're in the mess because of you—*it's your fault, David!*"

The Bible says that "the soul of all the people was *grieved*" (1 Sam. 30:6). They were grieved because of their painful circumstances. They felt helpless, and no relief was in sight! One of our greatest challenges in the Christian life is to *learn how not to get grieved when things go wrong.* God is determined to teach us how to look up in hard times like the Psalmist and say, "My help cometh from the Lord" (Ps. 121:2a)! We cannot afford to get caught up in circumstances. Are you worried about how you are going to make it next month or next year? You may be saying, "But I can't even handle today yet!" You may have a job, but you still worry and say, "What if they lay me off?"

...but **David encouraged himself in the Lord his God** (1 Samuel 30:6).

David did something we must learn to do. He "encouraged himself in the Lord." He remembered God's care and provision and recalled His goodness and power. We need to learn to "encourage ourselves" because sometimes there won't be anybody else to do it! David could not go to his friends for encouragement—they were busy collecting rocks to stone him. He couldn't go to his wives; they had been taken captive. *He had no one to help him.*

Improve Your Hearing: Be Encouraged

Do you realize that you can't hear the voice of God until you "get encouraged"? Whether you are a pastor, a mother, a business person, or a military commander, you are still human. In times of crisis—even though you have the responsibility and the authority to "find some way to turn around the situation," you still need to "be encouraged in the Lord" before you can hear His solution! You must learn how to encourage yourself in the Lord. We can sit in church and listen to great preaching and teaching for a century, but when a crisis invades our lives, if we are full of frustration, we cannot really hear God's voice.

What did David do first when the "Ziklag crisis" destroyed his world? After he freely expressed his human pain, he didn't call a council together. He didn't summon his committee or call all his friends. He went straight to the Source of all joy and encouragement. He encouraged himself *in the Lord*! If we can't encourage ourselves in Him, then why should we listen to Him? If we fail to encourage, reassure, and remind ourselves of His love and matchless ability to save, then we will never hear His words! Frustration, doubt, and unbelief will reduce even the deepest wisdom to "platitudes" in our eyes if we don't encourage ourselves in God.

Sprinkle "What" on My Door?!

Israel couldn't hear God's clear promise of deliverance when Moses tried to prophesy to them because of their terrible "anguish of spirit" and "cruel bondage" (Ex. 6:9). When we do finally hear God's voice, we always discover that the solution requires *faith*. God told the children of Israel to take the blood of a lamb and sprinkle it over their doors so the death angel (the problem) would pass them by. They could not say, "Well, I don't believe it." They had to put it over their door in faith and find out. In the same way, we must begin to praise God and trust Him to work things out for our good. Like the Israelites, we will see His great power deliver us and bring us out. You know how God brought them out? They believed on the blood that was over that door. They believed that the blood over the door would protect them.

We have to believe that the blood that He shed will protect us. We must believe that when we confess that we have been made whole, that His wholeness is ours. We must believe it to experience it. If we are full of frustration, then we can't hear godly advice.

The things with which we fill our hearts will come out in our conversation. As we read God's Word, our hearts, thoughts, and words will change. We must learn to praise God in all things and keep Him ever on our minds. Isaiah said, "Thou [God] wilt keep him in perfect peace, whose mind is stayed on [fixed on] Thee: because he trusteth in Thee" (Is. 26:3).

What Are You Sowing in Your Children?

The enemy wants our families to see us respond negatively in times of disappointment and stress. He wants to destroy the next generation by making them "barren." When we allow bitterness, unforgiveness, and selfishness to rule our marriage relationship, we cause our children to vow, "I don't ever want to get married." Our poor example can rob our children of productivity and hope for a joyful and abundant life. On the other hand, when we subject our marriages, personality weaknesses, and insecurities to Jesus Christ, we plant hope and reassurance in our childrens' hearts. We sow life into the next generation!

Freedom from frustration begins when we admit we have a problem. We have to stop saying, "But it's someone else's fault!" We have to say, "It's me, O Lord." That is why I advise couples who are dating to watch how their partners respond when they get upset or face crises. We should never think we "know" a people until we have seen them under pressure or in stressful circumstances.

God is here to set us free if we will trust Him, praise Him, and encourage ourselves in His faithfulness! Too often, when we run into problems and become frustrated, we say, "I don't care what you say—you can talk to me or preach God's way to me—but when I leave, I will still choose my own way" (see Prov. 14:12). Scripture does *not* say that "the just shall live by *circumstances* and give in to *frustration*." No, it says we have to live by *faith* (see Rom. 1:17).

Symptoms of Frustration and Bitterness

When frustration sets in, we tend to criticize other people in the areas we have experienced the most injury. If we have troubled marriages or family relationships, we will usually believe the worst about other people's relationships. Even worse, if we have allowed bitterness to fester in our hearts, we won't be able to help ourselves—we will sow bitter seeds of discord into anyone who will listen! If you are dealing with a person who is still carrying these wounds, then gently and firmly tell them that you won't receive those seeds of bitterness. Tell them your spouse is not like that. Remember: Bitter people often try to enlist others in their bitter thought cycles.

People burdened with unhealed wounds often say, "None of those churches are right!" Beware: they are spilling bitterness onto you. Poison is running out of their untended wounds, and the enemy is trying to get you to swallow it so he can poison your spiritual bloodstream. Many bitter people say, "You don't understand—I've been wounded by another Christian! I've been wounded in the house of my friends" (see Zech. 13:6).

As we mature in Christ, we usually realize that God sometimes allows wounds to come to perfect and strengthen our faith, and to purge certain things from our lives. He closely watches our response in times of crisis (see Job 5:18), to see if we only love Him for what He *gives us,* or if we will continue to trust Him and walk in love—just because He is God. Jesus set the supreme example for us when He walked victoriously to His own painful death on the cross, heavily laden with great affliction.

Let Me Show You How to Handle a Wound!

Jesus Christ says, "I have been wounded also. Let Me show you what to do with your wounds. Don't cling to or nurse those hurt areas; rather, uncover them and allow Me to heal them." He showed us how to overcome bitterness (see Eph. 4:31-32; Heb. 12:14-15). Our response to a crisis cannot be based on our feelings or our short-term perceptions. What about tomorrow? What about next week? How will your response affect your children? How will your refusal to trust God—your refusal to "encourage yourself in Him"—affect their lives, and the lives of their children?

It seems like everyone's dilemma is different from those of other people. The truth is that when we rely on God, every problem becomes an important lesson and a stepping-stone for growth. If you got married just because you didn't want to be alone, but now you realize it was a mistake, *what have you learned* from your mistake? Although you have learned that loneliness is not a reason to get married, now you must learn how to give your marriage to the Lord and trust Him for a miracle!

Some people, like the crippled man at the pool of Bethesda, live with their pain for a lifetime. Yet when Jesus came on the scene, this man suddenly faced a new choice. He was thoroughly frustrated by that time. He basically told Jesus, "I don't have anybody to help me. Somebody is always jumping in front of me; they don't care about crippled people" (see Jn. 5:7). I believe he had gotten so frustrated that Jesus stepped in and said, "You need some help!"

But You Don't Know What It's Like!

When Jesus said, "I came to help you," perhaps the crippled man said, "Nobody else has helped me, so You probably won't either. I've been like this for 38 years, and I don't know if I will *ever* get better! Man, You just don't know what it is like down here!" Jesus *does* know how we feel. He was touched with all the feelings of our infirmities, and He knows what we're going through (see Heb. 4:15).

We are human beings, and we will make mistakes and experience failures. Jesus could have told him, "You didn't have to be like this for 38 years, but you've been so busy lying there complaining that someone else stepped in front of you and got the blessing."

I want to tell you something important: You can make it wherever God plants you. You can make it right where you are *if you'll just change your thinking*! Renew your mind in the Word. It will help you "think like God thinks"! If you have done all that you know to do, and the job you want still won't open up, then God might be saying, "Start your own business." He might be saying,

"Bring that dream into reality, and start in your kitchen or in your garage."

What did God say to Moses? He asked him, "What is in your hand?" Moses' answer went like this: "Just this rod—this shepherd's staff that I use to herd my sheep" (see Ex. 4:2). God may be asking you, "What is in your hand? Can you trust Me to use it to bless you and others?"

Seven Times a Winner

What do you need from God? What is keeping you from just making up your mind that you want it, then going after it and not letting anything stop you? Proverbs 24:16a says, "For a just man falleth seven times, and riseth up again." It doesn't matter how many times you fail. If you are righteous, you're going to get back up again!

And there was a woman there who for eighteen years had had an infirmity caused by a spirit (a demon of sickness). She was bent completely forward and utterly unable to straighten herself up or to look upward. And when Jesus saw her, He called [her to Him] and said to her, Woman, you are released from your infirmity! Then He laid [His] hands on her, and instantly she was made straight, and she recognized and thanked and praised God (Luke 13:11-13 AMP).

Are you under some bondage that has you so defeated and frustrated that you can't look up or go forward either? Jesus wants to *loose you* from your every "infirmity" or hindrance that has you bound. The Greek word translated as "loose" means "to dismiss; let depart; to separate; to divorce."[3]

Reject the Bitterness of Frustration

If you want to be healed and to mature in your walk with God, then don't carry your problems around. Release them and refuse to allow frustration to poison your life and the lives of future generations. Reject the bitterness that makes you ineffective. Protect your "game plan" for victorious living. As you praise God and encourage yourself in the Lord, you will rise up above the problems, receive your miracle, and be loosed from the "infirmity" that has kept you defeated!

You and your seed (your natural or spiritual children) are a frightening threat to the devil when you allow God to turn your frustration into joy. The devil knows God will use your *healed* wounds to show other people how they too can be raised up and healed of every wound that has "arrested, captured, and seized" them! (Remember, the Greek word for "bitterness" means "to be arrested, captured or seized.")

Your scars prove you've survived the same situation those people are facing. God established David's kingdom forever because he was willing to let go of wounds and bitterness and be healed (see 2 Chron. 7:17-18). You can change your life and future generations if you release your frustration and let God turn your wounds to scars of victory!

End Notes

1. *Strong's Concordance,* definition of *maoz,* #4581 (Hebrew).

2. Merriam Webster's Collegiate Dictionary, p. 470.

3. *Strong's Concordance,* selected segments of definition #650 (Hebrew), *apoluo.*

Chapter 3

Facing Adversity and Healing Life's Hurts

Many of the people who file into our churches every week are desperately in need of some "spiritual therapy" to free them from the hurts of past failures and adversities. They need to get rid of the things that are holding them back so they can move on into what God wants for their lives. Perhaps you have recognized some things from your past that are hindering your own spiritual growth even as you read these words.

One of our problems is that we haven't understood the importance of *dealing* with these hurts. Have you noticed the different ways people react to the cry of a little baby? Adults who have no children, or whose children have grown up, often react with irritation. All they hear is a *noisy disturbance.* The child's parent, however, hears a *warning,* a cry for help, an unmistakable message that signals the existence of a problem! Sometimes we have a problem perceiving the *real* problem behind the warning signs in our lives and those around us. We still don't know how to recognize or deal with past hurts and failures.

Good Pastors Produce Victorious Sheep

As pastors, part of our role in the Body of Christ is to bring people to greater spiritual maturity and understanding in these areas. We know we have succeeded any time our sheep are able to stare adversity in the face and declare, "I have the victory in Christ!" This is positive proof they are making great strides toward maturity.

When you can stand in the middle of a situation that "hasn't worked out as you had planned," when you can face your failure squarely and declare in faith: "Things will work out! God will make a way. It may take awhile, but I believe God is working things out for my good!"—then you are truly moving forward.

The best way to recover from an injury and walk in victory and joy is to confront it! The Bible tells us exactly how to defeat our "giants" in the Book of First Samuel. David was just a teenager when he confronted Goliath, the giant warrior who had threatened Israel and paralyzed an entire army with fear and doubt. Goliath was so confident in his power that he taunted Israel's army with a challenge to man-to-man combat, hoping to take the entire nation captive for Philistia.

"And [David] took his staff in his hand, and chose him five smooth stones out of the brook, and put them in a shepherd's bag which he had, even in a scrip; and his sling was in his hand: and he drew near to the Philistine" (1 Sam. 17:40). God didn't send a mighty warrior onto the battlefield to meet the giant; He sent a boy with a tender heart.

The Fivefold Weapons of God

The staff David carried into combat with the giant symbolized the anointing of God, as well as the strength and guidance it provides. The five smooth stones in his shepherd's bag represented the "fivefold ministry" (the apostle, prophet, evangelist, pastor, and teacher). Their "rough edges" had been smoothed by the water (of God's Word) washing over them for years. They "waited in the Word" for the day of battle. It was no accident that God sent a shepherd—David's calling symbolizes Christ and true biblical eldership.

Every one of us who feels overwhelmed or insufficient for a challenge should take heart when we see how David defeated Goliath the giant. He prevailed *because he knew God,* and *because he trusted His Word* completely. Because David confronted the giant solely through the strength and guidance of the Holy Spirit's anointing, he came through victorious. If your hurts, wounds, and shortcomings look like giants too, you can overcome them by trusting God and His promises just as David did!

Some of us today, like doubting Thomas, say, "I won't believe until I see." Jesus told Thomas in John 20:29, "...because thou hast seen Me, thou hast believed: blessed are they that have not seen, and yet have believed." We believe He is still telling us today, "You are to walk and live by faith and trust in Me, and you are especially blessed when you believe before you see the evidence!"

You Are Under a Debtor's Decree!

Jesus revealed an eternal principle in "the Lord's prayer" while teaching His disciples to pray. He said, "And forgive us our debts, as we forgive our debtors"

(Mt. 6:12). Every time we pray those words, we declare a contract and a covenant that says, in essence, *"Father, only forgive me if I forgive the person who did wrong to me"*! With this prayer, we've made a contract with God—and He's a covenant-keeping God. We today have many problems because we lack knowledge of His ways and His covenants (see Hos. 4:6).

The laws of God, like the lesser laws of the physical world, remain the same whether we understand them or not. Our ignorance doesn't suspend the law of gravity. If you jump out of an airplane, you will fall to the earth—even if you do not understand how it works! In the same way, the laws and principles of God work whether we understand them or not. The moment we pray, "Our Father which art in heaven...*forgive us our debts, as we forgive our debtors,*" we enter into a covenant with God that states we won't be forgiven unless we forgive others. We essentially say, "Don't send any blood to heal my wounded mind if I'm still holding bitterness against others." Perhaps we didn't understand at the time what we were saying, but it still remains an immutable law.

It Takes the Blood to Clean the Stain

We will never experience healing without the spiritual blood of the Lamb rushing in to cleanse us. When we walk around "spewing out bitterness" and poisoning the lives of others; when we say, "There's no love in churches; those people don't care anymore," then we have exempted ourselves from forgiveness! The Bible says:

A father of the fatherless, and a judge of the widows, is God in His holy habitation. God setteth the solitary in families: He bringeth out those which are bound with chains: but the rebellious dwell in a dry land (Psalm 68:5-6).

God takes the solitary and puts them into families. He didn't make any of us an island. The family was never meant to be a place where people hate and mistreat others—that is not a family, it is just a bunch of people living together outside of God's covenant!

God declares, "...whatsoever a man soweth, that shall he also reap" (Gal. 6:7). If you are sowing love, then people will love you. It's God's spiritual law. It never fails. You can't sow love and not get it back, or God would be a liar, and God cannot lie (see Tit. 1:2). If you're loving others, it is a mandate from Heaven that you are loved. If you feel unloved, then there is possibly a wounded area in your life that you have not recognized or dealt with by placing it under the blood of Jesus.

God gave us a wonderful invitation and promise of restoration in the Book of Isaiah when He declared, "Ho, every one that thirsteth, come ye to the waters..." (Is. 55:1). This isn't the only time our Maker has called us "to the waters." The Church was birthed in the river of Living Water flowing from God's Son! Jesus Christ met the Samaritan woman at the well and offered her *living water*: "But whosoever drinketh of the water that I shall give him shall never thirst; but *the water that I shall give him shall be in him a well of water* springing up into everlasting life" (Jn. 4:14).

We Want That "Special" Water

Although the woman was a failure and an adulterer, she dared to believe and receive the words of Jesus, and her life was changed. Then she preached the good news, and many of the people in her town "came to the waters" as well! There is something special about those waters that brings washing, cleansing, and restoration to even the worst of souls! Your ability or right to the "living water" of God doesn't depend on how much money you have or who you are. All of us have a free invitation to receive His living water, the milk of the Word, and the wine of the Spirit. We need to learn that God works out all things according to His good plan for our lives (see Rom. 8:28). If we have "come to the waters," then supernatural faith has been birthed in us!

Jesus knew that Peter would face a terrible crisis in the courtyard of the high priest, and He also knew Peter would fail by denying Him before men. Jesus told Peter something that *we need to hear* today, and He prophesied it *before* it happened:

*And the Lord said, Simon, Simon, behold, Satan hath desired to have you, that he may sift you as wheat: but I have prayed for thee, that thy faith fail not: and **when thou art converted**, strengthen thy brethren* (Luke 22:31-32).

We Are "Under Conversion"

Conversion is a *process* of renewal. Salvation takes place instantly in the heart, but conversion starts in the mind. Conversion means "to change the thinking or opinion, to go in a different direction." When we receive Jesus Christ as Lord and Savior, we cannot continue to operate according to our old thought patterns. Many of us haven't come to greater maturity because we are trying to work spiritual truths with carnal, unrenewed minds! We are thinking like the worldly kingdom while trying to live in God's Kingdom—it just won't work.

In God's Kingdom, those who humble themselves will be exalted, while those who exalt themselves will be brought down (see Mt. 23:12). We "exalt ourselves" by trying to do things our own way (which is actually the world's way). We "humble ourselves" by choosing to do things God's way. There is a big difference between our way and God's way!

Psalm 19:7 says, "The law of the Lord is perfect, converting the soul...." God's Word contains all the instruction and teaching we need to change our old thought processes. Our spirit-man is already converted and made perfect, *but not our soul.* (The "soul" includes the mind, thoughts, will, and emotions.) When your soul is *converted,* your mind, your will, and your emotions will also be changed or turned around.

Converting the Anxious Majority

Your thoughts control and change your actions. Even though you are born again, there are still occasions when you will react to situations in the "old way." When you have thoughts and reactions that aren't godly, then you know you are not fully "converted" in that area. Do you still get upset when people gossip about you? Do you still worry about money and miss sleep anticipating a large bill coming due? You are not alone. Most of us are still anxious about many things, and we know we need to be converted and change our thinking in this area to conform to God's Word.

The "renewal of the mind" is a learning and growing process. It doesn't happen overnight. It occurs over time as we seek God, study His Word, and remain sensitive to His dealings. The first step to renewing the mind is to "consume" the Word of God. We need to read it, speak it, and meditate on it daily. To "meditate" means to "chew on it" like we chew gum. When we think about God's Word and continually apply it to our own experiences, it will take root deep inside our spirits, and we will discover that even our *thought patterns* will begin to change! We'll no longer feel the same about things, and often we won't even be able to pinpoint when we changed.

David cried out to God, "Restore unto me the joy of Thy salvation.... Then will I teach transgressors Thy ways; and sinners shall be converted unto Thee" (Ps. 51:12-13). Does your joy evaporate when frustration and aggravation come? Call out to God like David did. When you are full of joy, you will be a help to the Body of Christ and a threat to the devil's domain!

Afflictions Are "Standard Equipment"

We need to stop expecting life to be problem-free! It may come as a surprise to you, but things will never work out exactly as you want them to. In Psalm 34:19, the Psalmist said, "Many are the afflictions [problems] of the righteous...." In the same breath, he says, "...but the Lord delivereth him out of them all"! God is strengthening us as we trust and rejoice in Him—even in the midst of the problems. He is restoring our joy, and now it is time for us to "teach transgressors His ways"!

It is "hunting season"! It's "fishing season" in the spiritual realm. Now that you have received your "fishing license," you need to go fishing for the souls of the lost in your own house, job site, and city. Seek out those who are bound by drug addiction, alcoholism, and all the other enticements of satan. Bring them to Jesus and help them with the power God has given you as His child!

First you need to free yourself from all the hurts and bondages of your past. You need to convert and change your thinking so you can look at them and say, "I used to have terrible problems, but not anymore. God has restored me! He even changed how I feel about things." Sinners will be converted to God and the devil's strongholds will fall when we become walking testimonials of His great joy!

Don't Quit Until God "Changes Your Name"

Have you ever wanted something so much that you just wouldn't give up? Do you desire God's best so strongly that you refuse to quit? Jacob was like that. He had a lot of problems and personality flaws, but he kept pressing into God the best way he knew. In the biggest crisis of his life, he wrestled with the angel of God all night—he just would not give up! If Jacob had not been willing to push on and persevere through the all-night wrestling match, he might never have been "converted."

Jacob emerged from the contest with a victory that changed his life—he had encountered God, and now his name (and his destiny) was changed! He was no longer Jacob—one who supplants or deceives. God said he was now Israel—a prince who has power with God. God uses our struggles to help us grow out of our deadly "Jacob mind-set." He wants each of us to become "Israels" who are spiritual giants and examples to others!

When adversity grips you and won't let go, just look that problem in the face and declare that God will bring you out and bring you through! Declare: "Whether this problem lets go of me or not, I won't give up. I'm going to walk in the blessings of God!"

One problem is that wounded people often say, "Nobody tells me what to do!" Authority figures in their lives have so abused and misused them that they have rebelled against *all* authority—including the authority of God. The wonderful truth is that God is still able to heal and restore even the most wounded areas of our lives if we will open our hearts to Him. We need to make God's words and ways the main priority in our lives: "Incline your ear, and come unto Me: hear, and your soul shall live; and I will make an everlasting covenant with you, even the sure mercies of David" (Is. 55:3). God has promised victory in every area of life if we allow our thoughts to be converted and renew our minds.

God "Puts Our Head on Straight"

Some of us still think like unrighteous wicked men, but God says, "Let the wicked forsake his way, and the unrighteous man his thoughts" (Is. 55:7a). A sinner who gets upset or faces a problem may say, "I'll get drunk or do some drugs—it'll numb my mind for a little while...." When the Holy Spirit fills us, we are no longer troubled by what used to bother us. An alcoholic may use a drink to forget his problems for awhile, but we can rely on the Holy Spirit to take us *through* our problems. We can cast all our cares on the Lord and release our frustrations to Him so we can be healed (see 1 Pet. 5:7).

If we accept God's invitation to "come to the waters," then we will "go out with joy, and be led forth with peace" (Is. 55:12). His peace surpasses all understanding, and it will even guide us in our daily decisions (see Phil. 4:7; Col. 3:15)! If we don't have a sense of His peace in a matter or decision, we know that God is not in it.

Do you long to "know Him, and the power of His resurrection"? (Phil. 3:10) In the Greek, "to know" means "to know by experience." We rejoice in His faithfulness because we know that even in our darkest disappointments, the power of His resurrection will bring life and healing. We can remain confident that He will bring us through every storm of life because God has a good plan for us (see Jer. 29:10). The apostle Paul wrote:

> *Brethren, I count not myself to have apprehended* [I'm not what I should be]*: but this one thing I do, forgetting those things which are behind* [in the past]*, and reaching forth unto those things which are before, I press toward the mark for the prize of the high calling of God in Christ Jesus* (Philippians 3:13-14).

This is the key to facing adversity and overcoming faults and past hurts! If we concentrate on our pain and the people who mistreated and abused us, we will forget what Jesus accomplished for us by the power of His shed blood and resurrection! Just as you are ready to step forward into your calling, your past will yank on that "rope" and holler, "Hey! You're forgetting all your hurt! You'll get hurt again!"

You Can't Look Up When You're Looking Down

Paul said he was going to "totally forget" the things of the past. He turned his attention away from the pain of the past and riveted his attention to his high calling. He said he was going to "press toward the mark." The Greek word for "press" means "to pursue." We can't pursue anything if we are always nursing our wounds!

Have you vowed to never let anyone hurt you the way they hurt you or members of your family in the past? Have you become hard? Has it put you so far from the things of God that you feel like a "spiritual icicle"? Is there really any wound so grievous or person so important that you would allow it or him to keep you from the presence of your God? God is urging us to "press toward the mark [the target] for the prize of the high calling" (Phil. 3:14). It will never happen if your eyes are focused on your hurts!

Deliverance always requires obedience. I've known people who rejected God's healing saying, "The last time I got a word, it didn't come to pass." My first thought is: "Did you do exactly what God said last time?" The answer is almost always *no*! By now we should know that God engineers many of our circumstances to strengthen us in the faith—He doesn't tempt us with evil, but He is determined to help us better understand His ways and teach us the enemy's tactics. If you are "resisting and rebuking the devil" and nothing has changed, you may be surprised to discover that the hand of God is in them. He may be the Master Architect of your difficulty, yet you can be sure that His master plan includes a way to take you through and make you more like Jesus!

God works all things for our good (see Rom. 8:28). He cares and provides for us in every situation, and He is not frivolous. We are not mere pawns on His cosmic chessboard; we are sons and daughters of His delight! God is Sovereign, and He has an eternal plan that we may not always understand, but we can trust Him, for *God is good* (see Ps. 143:10; Mt. 19:17; Mk. 10:18; Lk. 18:19).

Don't Let Him Wear You Out

If you trust and rely on God, you will see His power and grace in your circumstances, and your faith will increase. Release your frustrations, hurts, and bitterness to Him, and learn to forgive. Be on guard against the enemy's devices and his persistent attacks. In Daniel 7:25, the prophet warns us that the devil will come to "wear out the saints." He works his devious plans little by little, over a period of time. However, if we seek God, we won't be "unaware of satan's devices."

People don't get married, have one bad day, and decide to get a divorce. They allow frustration and bitterness to *gradually* grow and develop until they say, "I don't want to be married to you anymore." Samson revealed the secret of his strength to Delilah only after she *continuously pressed and pushed him*, using the love he had for her as leverage. The enemy wants you to love the things that are not good for you. (If Samson hadn't loved Delilah, he never would have trusted her.) Delilah's name means "oppression, to make thin or narrow, to empty out, to impoverish."[1] She wore down Samson's resistance until he reached a breaking point. Because of her seduction and betrayal, Samson lost his great strength. His eyes were plucked out and he became the slave of his enemies. He was literally "emptied out" and "utterly impoverished."

God's voice is rarely loud. Yet the heart that desires to hear His voice above all things will hear Him clearly—in spite of the enemy's clamor. There is no problem too large, no hurt so deep, and no voice so loud that God cannot make Himself heard.

Don't Blame Tonto!

Unfortunately, some of us are spiritual "lone rangers." We try to work everything out by ourselves, becoming more frustrated and confused day by day. Then we are easily convinced that nobody cares and that their talk of love and caring is just a pretense. We will read rejection into every look. We may even think they are talking about us and laughing at us. No one can tell us it isn't so because we "know what we saw"!

The enemy loves to separate believers from the Body of Christ to nurse such grievances as this. He whispers to their minds, "You can handle this on your own. Just work it out by yourself. Don't trust them; remember—they'll only hurt you." If this sounds familiar, then watch out! If we stay in fellowship and reject the devil's lies, we can discern his confusing tongue and cruel deception.

Most of us don't understand the power of fellowship. The Lord urges us in Hebrews 10:24-25: "And let us consider one another to provoke unto love...not forsaking the assembling [gathering] of ourselves together...." If we would share our thoughts and frustrations with the Body and ask for help, we wouldn't get stuck in the vicious thought-cycle of fear and rejection the enemy has fed us.

A few of us think we are "super-saints"! If someone asks, "How are you?" We may be near death, but we feel we have to answer, "Great! Praise God, I couldn't be better!" Why? We are afraid that if we ever admit we have a problem, people will think we're not "spiritual." As we exhibit true faith and peace in our lives through Jesus, we will win the world. Yet, it is equally important that we be transparent and show genuine care for each other when we come together.

Our Doctor Makes House Calls

God knows where you are and what you've done. We all have frailties and faults, and we're all at different levels of understanding and spiritual growth. He is merciful. He works with each of us right where we are—He makes house calls! He is quick to speak to us and bless us in spite of our problems, failures, and misconceptions. For this reason, we shouldn't be so quick to judge others. God wants to heal us from the hurts of the past and the frustrations of wrong choices and difficult circumstances as His Word cleanses us, restores our souls, and converts our thinking.

When life hands us problems, we must not focus on our wounds. We should trust God to bring healing and victory. If we've allowed hardness to imprison our heart, we need to let God remove that hardness so we can once again become teachable and pliable in His hands. It is time for us to forget past hurts and focus our eyes on the target! We must "press toward the mark for the prize of the high calling of God" and pursue His best and highest plan for our lives!

End Note

1. *Strong's Concordance,* definition #1807, #1809 (Hebrew).

Chapter 4

Dealing With Offenses and Failure

And ye shall know the truth, and the truth shall make you free (John 8:32).

Statistics have shown that when children experience things that are very distressing to them, they have a tendency to suppress or "block out" their painful memories. We all tend to conceal our most painful hurts deep in our subconscious, where they are hidden even from ourselves. When they resurface as sore spots in our marriages and other areas of adult life—we don't know what is wrong! If we continue to ignore or suppress our pain and wounded memories, we will never be able to "forget" the past and be released from our pain.

Don't Hide Your Need

Socrates said, "To thine own self be true." This is true in the sense that we must not hide from the things that are inside us. Don't hide your need to be whole! If you are not aware of the truth about your needs, fears, wounds, or shortcomings, you can never get free from the bondage they produce in your life! If you won't admit you are wrong, you can never repent of or turn away from it. When you go before God while suppressing or repressing certain memories or thoughts, then you are approaching Him with everything *but* the truth. (He sees them anyway, no matter how deeply you have buried your secrets.)

You know you still have bitterness and pain in your heart when you notice that you always drag the names of other people with you into the presence of God, *so you can blame them* for your problems! Do you catch yourself pinning the blame for your "rotten life" on your parents, your spouse, your children, your pastor, or your boss? You need God's help to uncover the suppressed or repressed things from your past, or you will never be able to confess the *truth*: "I am the real problem, Lord. I need help!"

Do you secretly (or not so secretly) hate your mother for the way she "smothered" you as a child? Maybe that is why, as an adult, you despise anyone who tries to give you affection—you feel like that person is "smothering" you too! God created us as marvelously complex creatures, with an almost unlimited capacity to feel, to think, and to dream. Abuse, misuse, and sin can create equally complex problems and pain within us.

It's More Than "Kid's Stuff"

Many times your feelings have nothing to do with the person you are dealing with in the present—the emotions you feel may be connected to painful events from your childhood! This isn't "psychology"; it is Bible *truth* that was "discovered" by psychologists after the fact. The Bible is full of references to people who were bound by physical, spiritual, and social problems in childhood—including Jacob, Joseph, the man Jesus healed at the pool of Bethesda, the lame man healed by the disciples at the Gate Beautiful, and the paralytic man who was lowered to Jesus through a hole in the roof.

> *Follow peace with all men, and holiness, without which no man shall see the Lord: looking diligently lest any man fail of the grace of God; lest any* **root of bitterness** *springing up trouble you, and thereby many be defiled* (Hebrews 12:14-15).

Major problems always have a beginning and a source of pain. If you never allow the Holy Spirit to reveal them, and confess the truth about them and deal with them, then they will become roots of bitterness in your life. In the end they may destroy you! Even worse, they may spread their evil roots into your little boys' or little girls' lives!

Sometimes we experience things that are so painful that we don't want to face them. When your mental agony reaches that point, you will probably bury your emotions and memories. How many people are brave enough to stand up and say, "I have buried this problem and all the emotions that came with it—but truthfully, I hated my mother, and I despised my father! Frankly, any mention of God gets on my nerves. I just don't want to hear about God right now!"

Our Own Private Hell

We have known of people who never dealt with their past. Because they were never able to release all their hurt and hatred, in their bitterness, they even cursed God on their deathbed! Most people just aren't brave enough to say these things. The sad reality is that we will *forever* build walls around our hearts that will *keep love and healing from reaching us* unless we learn to be honest with God and ourselves. This sure sounds like a pretty good definition of "hell" to us!

When we frantically run and hide things from ourselves and other people, we eventually become very confused. We have difficulty dealing with reality, and we may begin to wonder "who we really are" or which part of us is the "real" person. That makes it easy to place blame on everyone but ourselves, and to become critical fault-finders.

Vernette: God Said, "Deal With *You!*"

Years ago, early in our marriage, I told the Lord in prayer, "Lord, *if my husband* would only do this, or say that...then I would be happy." I was always telling God what my husband *wasn't* doing right. God quickly helped me get to the root of my problem! He said, "Your husband is not the source of your unhappiness. Even if he held your hand all day, kissed you every time he got near you, sent you flowers every week, and said nice things to you all the time, *you still wouldn't be happy!*" God showed me that there was something in *me* that needed to be dealt with. He was telling me, *"Deal with you! Help yourself."*

Then I asked Him what part of my life I needed to examine and deal with. He sent a prophet to me who said, "God said something happened in your childhood." That's all he said. "Something happened in your childhood." *Well, thanks a lot!* It really aggravated me. I was thinking, **What** *happened in my childhood? I can think of a billion things that happened in my childhood, God! You've helped me a whole lot—thank You!* Now I felt more confused than I was before I prayed. I was totally aggravated and frustrated. Then I went to God again and prayed, "You mentioned my childhood, Lord. Please show me what You meant."

I began to entreat God, and this time I let the Holy Spirit do His job. He uncovered the *hidden thing*; He revealed to me the exact root of the place that I needed to deal with at that time. You know, God is "a discerner of the thoughts and intents of the heart" (Heb. 4:12). He knows just what we need in every realm of life, if we will just go to Him in faith and ask for His help and wisdom.

Coattail Happiness Is Temporary

If you don't know where you need help, you won't be able to confess it and confront it. If you don't confess your problem or pain, then you can never get forgiveness or release from it. Then you will constantly find bitter roots and unforgiveness springing up in your life. You will never be able to be all God wants you to be. You will always be expecting somebody else to make you happy and whole. You will always be trying to ride to contentment on someone else's coattails. God wants you to learn to be happy in yourself, and in who He made you to be.

If your happiness is dependent on somebody else, you will always live on an emotional roller-coaster of hurt and rejection. However, when your joy springs from your relationship with Jesus Christ, then no matter what anyone else does, your river of joy and life will spring up and flow with abundance. You won't be controlled by the actions or inaction of others. Freedom and wholeness begin when you begin to honestly face the *truth* about your problems and your past. It is not God's will that you run or hide from your pain—He wants you to stand up and confront those situations!

We must face "what once was" so we can live in *wholeness* in "what is now" and "what will be" in the future. Someone may have abused you, or perhaps you suffered through the pain of cruel rejection. It may seem that relationships have never worked out for you. Perhaps you are one of the millions of people who have been hurt in a church, and now you are suspicious of all churches and church people. Maybe you knew a preacher who lacked integrity and bitterly disappointed you. No matter what thing from the past is binding you emotionally, physically, or spiritually, you must recognize it and deal with it to be free!

The Guilt of the "Guiltless"

Guilt is one of the greatest problems that people fail to overcome. Children who have been sexually molested often associate deep guilt with any physical pleasure they may have felt during the episodes of abuse. They don't understand that those feelings of sexual pleasure were purely an automatic *biological response* triggered against their will—they are blaming themselves for something that is *not their fault.*

The self-worth of abuse victims is diminished as they experience deep feelings of guilt and shame, even though they were merely innocent victims. This can lead to the development of a "martyr-syndrome" where they blame everyone else for the problems in their lives in later years. Their adult life may be punctuated by constant complaints that no one appreciates or loves them, and nobody recognizes their worth. They often feel lonely and they think people are always trying to take advantage of them.

The truth is that we all feel those things when there are deeply rooted problems from our past that have not been dealt with. No one is really "out to get us" or make us feel unloved or unappreciated. Those feelings emanate from our wounded hearts and minds. If we don't get to the root of our problem and face ourselves, we will never come to God with the truth!

Don't come to God by trying to manipulate Him into doing things your way, and don't try to make people treat you a certain way. That isn't confession; that's lying! If you have used manipulation to get what you want from others, you need to confess it. Manipulation only inflicts more wounds! Allow the Holy Spirit to uncover the truth—the root of the problem—then when you deal with it you can walk in freedom from those things that have damaged and controlled your life for so long.

Confront Your Accuser!

At some point we must be willing to confront people and situations, and even the enemy, to be completely liberated from the past. We must renew our minds and change our thinking to *speak God's promises rather than our problems.* Finally, we must turn around and chase the devil, and command him to take his filthy hands off every part of our lives! Otherwise, the devil will chase us through marriage after marriage, from job to job, and from church to church! Face him in the power and authority of Jesus Christ and say, "I refuse to move! This has happened before and I'm going to get it taken care of! I'm putting it under the blood and out of my system so it won't happen again!"

God is bringing us to a *point of confrontation* because He wants us to be honest with ourselves and with others (that's *confrontation*, not *fighting*). We are not to run people down, dissect their lives, or devour members of the Body of Christ with gossip and slandering tongues. No, He is calling us to godly, loving confrontation.

Christians often act like the most cowardly people in the world! We are wimps who are easily offended! It's a fact that "if you *can* be offended, you *will* be offended!" If the enemy gets you to stumble over someone's actions or attitude, he has rendered you ineffectual and unproductive!

Offense Is Tearing Apart the Church!

Pretense and unforgiveness are fueling the growing sense of offense in the Church today! What if you felt offended by someone in your church, and that person came to you to ask, "Did I offend you?" Would you piously answer, "Who, me? No! No, brother, you didn't offend me." (Many of us would.) When the person believes your pretense and turns away thinking he is forgiven, would you quickly find a sympathetic ear and say, "Oh! He gets on my nerves! I just don't like him. Did I ever tell you about…"?

The fact is that when a brother tries to repair an offense according to biblical guidelines, and you refuse to forgive, then *you have refused to face the truth*! Too many Christians are too proud to admit when they are offended. It doesn't matter how small a thing is that hurts your feelings—make up your mind to get it taken care of! Don't allow any offense to bring a root of bitterness into your life!

Some people are constantly offended because they *hold things on the inside*, rather than sharing their hurt with the offender or with a spiritual brother or sister who can pray with them and help them through it! Their futile efforts to "handle" everything by themselves often produces cancer, fatal heart attacks, or dangerous stress levels that in turn trigger debilitating strokes, migraine and stress headaches, and a myriad of other illnesses. These things are *body signals* warning us that we need to deal with some hidden roots. When your head hurts, your limbs go numb, or your heart palpitates—it may be your body saying, "Talk to someone about it! Recognize the pain and deal with it!"

Push the Release Valve

Many of us have a built-in "release valve" that faithfully warns us and those around us that we have a problem. These inner mechanisms keep us from exploding! Tears are a natural, physical release valve. The ability to communicate will release a great deal of pressure from our lives. God didn't make us to handle all this pressure *alone*. He made us social creatures who dwell in families (physical, spiritual, cultural, ethnic, and national "families"). We are divinely placed in the Body of Christ to help and strengthen each other.

We hold many things in because of our pride. Finally, we build up so much pressure that we just explode. We may say, "God told me to let all my anger out like this!" but God doesn't operate that way. Many of us would rather let pride hamper us and hold us back than *admit we have a problem*! For our part, we have had our share of battles with pride.

Vernette: He Wouldn't Let Me Run Anymore!

God had to keep telling me, "I won't let you be a turncoat in this ministry; I won't let you run. I will put you in a corner so you will have to fight your way out of it. Nobody will ever listen to you as long as you keep trying to avoid people who don't believe in women ministers or pastors! Stop worrying about what people think—stop being upset because people accuse you of favoritism!"

God reminded me that He had called me to be a "Deborah, a judge (or savior with a small 's')." I was to encourage and teach people so they could come out of darkness and be set free by the truth. *Now I am no longer in the running business!* I realized that running wouldn't make the problem just disappear some day.

Having four gifted children who flow with us in ministry, we have heard many accusations of "favoritism." I tried to "prove" to people that I could be "fair" while dealing with church members' children and my own children. I was even unfair to my own children at times—just to prove something to people *who already had their minds made up anyway*! They always assumed I would respond in the same biased way *they* would respond. (Try owning your own school and mix your children in with the rest of the students—that experience will definitely draw you closer to God!)

God spoke to me one day in the midst of my struggle, saying, "Stop letting people's opinions and comments control you. I didn't let you run from the ministry, and I won't let you *teach your children* to run either!" I made a decision one day and said, "By the grace of God, I won't deal with this anymore, because it doesn't trouble me anymore. I have done what I was supposed to do. I am not bothered."

God knew my heart—the opinions of others no longer controlled me in any way. I became more concerned with what God thought, and whether I was doing things right in His sight. Suddenly, that subject was no longer an issue. Some of us run from struggle or conflict, but when we contend for the *right thing*, we focus attention on the good things we bring to businesses, marriage relationships, and every other thing we are involved in. People are less likely to take advantage of those who are outspoken and unafraid of controversy!

Don't Circle the Mountain Twice!

We have entered a special season of grace when God is bringing complete healing and restoration to the wounded areas of our lives. Now is the time to face these things and deal with them. If we refuse, we will not be able to move on with our lives and we will stop growing in Him. Trust Him to bring you into the promised land, or you will wander aimlessly through the desert places in pointless circles. Don't hold back, or you might end up in the same place on the mountain that you were ten years ago!

It is time to deal with the hidden hindrances in our personal lives and ministries. We must have personal integrity and allow the Holy Spirit to create the character of Christ within us. We cannot ride on another person's coattails any longer! If we refuse to confront immediate situations, healing will never come. Now, we have no right to devastate people when we confront them; so all our actions are to be dictated by the love and compassion of the Holy Spirit. He will lead us into truth and give us wisdom to handle every situation.

Don't Fear Failure: Learn From It!

Every great leader in the Bible and even in human history seems to have been well acquainted with *failure*. Even Jesus Christ—*in the eyes of the onlooking world and the devil*—had failed when He died on the cross. Their mistake was in underestimating the wisdom and power of God. The shed blood and death of Jesus were the very means God used to redeem us from death and hell! (And you *know* what followed the cross!)

Most of us have refused to step out and tackle certain challenges or opportunities as children and adults *because we are afraid to fail*! Yet God uses our failures to accomplish His will as much as He uses our successes! Consider Abraham (who disobeyed God by taking along Lot, and pretending Sarah wasn't his wife); Jacob (the deceiver and supplanter); Joseph the dreamer (who unwisely bragged of his promotion over his brothers that he saw in a dream); Moses (the murderer); Jonah (and his "fish" story); Samson (the womanizer); David (the adulterer and murderer); and Elijah (who ran from one angry woman after he had called down the fire of God and killed the priests of Baal).

In the New Testament, think of Peter (who denied Jesus); the Samaritan woman at the well (who was living in sin); John Mark (who abandoned Paul and Barnabas); and Paul (who murdered Christians in the name of religion).

You Must Fail in Order to Succeed!

In the world of modern sports, the greatest athletes are always those who take great risks (and often fail) to achieve new heights. The top "home run hitters" of all time *also* accumulated more *strikeouts* than any other group of professional baseball players! Also, the mistakes and failures of great leaders always affect more people than those of lesser men and women. Consider David. His disobedient decision to "number" Israel cost 70,000 innocent lives by the time he finally realized his sin, confessed it, and made his heart right with God (see 2 Sam. 24:15).

Failure isn't bad—it is a natural part of the process that produces success in our lives! Abraham Lincoln experienced 29 long years of failure in his bid for high political office. If he and others before him—who didn't have the revelation and understanding of God's resources we have today—managed to overcome decades of failure, how much more can we overcome and prevail in this day?

In 1831, Abraham Lincoln went bankrupt. In 1832, he failed again. Most of us would have said, "That's it. I'm out of here." The very next year, Mr. Lincoln failed again.

The following year, he suffered a nervous breakdown! Surely he said, "I'm definitely quitting now!" No, he recovered from the nervous breakdown only to be miserably beaten in a political race! Every time Abraham Lincoln experienced failure, he learned to do something *right* the next time!

Is Failure Really Good?

If you have ever experienced defeat, you may appreciate Lincoln a little more after this: Lincoln was defeated again in a bid for a seat in Congress, but he didn't give up. He was beaten *twice* when he ran for the office of Vice President of the United States, and he also lost a race for a seat in the U.S. Senate! It seems like he just wouldn't learn—or did he have a different understanding of failure? Would he ever get "sensible" and just give up? No. Abraham Lincoln had a goal, and he refused to stop moving forward—no matter how many times he fell backwards. The next time he ran for political office he actually won—he was inaugurated as the sixteenth President of the United States in 1861 at the age of 52!

Abraham Lincoln endured nearly three decades of frustration and humiliating defeat, *but he didn't let it stop him*! In the end, he finally became the President of the United States, and led the nation through the most dangerous and difficult conflict in its short history! Those years of perseverance in the face of opposition uniquely equipped Lincoln to lead America through the violent upheaval of the Civil War! In the same way, David's difficult years as a "failure and fugitive" avoiding the armies of King Saul helped prepare him for the day he would assume the throne of Judah and Israel. Is there an individual or a nation waiting for you to complete your "failure" training so you can lead them to success?

Uh Oh—Stop the World!

Have you ever "wallowed in self-pity" and asked, "Why me?" We need to understand the biblical principles concerning freedom and restoration from the failures of the past. Don't let past failures make you give up or stop moving forward. Never allow your past to have more control over you than the nature of Jesus Christ within you! The world won't grind to a stop just because you have tried something twice and failed! Don't give in to the human tendency to focus on the bad instead of the good! Avoid the selfish tendency to be self-centered and to concentrate only on your hurts and wounds.

Selfish people love the words *always* and *never*, and especially the word *me*. They love the phrase, "You *never* do anything for *me*. You *always* ignore *my* needs!" Selfish people don't remember the good things they've received from other people and from God because they're focused on themselves. All they can see are the frustrations and failures from their past.

Don't Waste Your Trials!

Do you view trouble and hardships in the wrong way? Have you ever quit doing what God told you to do just because you failed along the way? Do you lose interest in the things of God if everything doesn't go the way you expected? Have you "gone on strike" because somebody hurt you, and are you refusing to do anything for God because you were "mistreated"? God's Word says trials come to develop our faith in Him!

Wherein ye greatly rejoice, though now for a season, if need be, ye are in heaviness through manifold temptations: that the trial of your faith, being much more precious than of gold that perisheth, though it be tried with fire, might be found unto praise and honour and glory at the appearing of Jesus Christ (1 Peter 1:6-7).

Every time we stand and trust God to bring us through a difficult time, that trial builds the character of God in us. It makes our confidence in God unshakable! God is making you into His image. Stop looking at your problem and thinking God hates you! He is trying to teach you to rely on Him. When you start regarding trials as an opportunity to trust God and develop greater faith, you will be able to help others learn to depend on Him too!

The Limbo of "Arrested Development"

It saddens us to see people delayed or stopped by their past—they are in a state of spiritual "arrested development." They are stuck in the limbo of the past, not growing, not thriving, and not maturing. God is calling all of us to break free from the past and come out of bondage! If you want to press into God, then you must make up your mind that you will be all God wants you to be—whatever the cost!

Don't allow your past to hinder your present. Don't let your "used to be" control your "now"! If you have allowed the hurts and wounds of your past to delay your ministry, then you are not where God wants you to be. If you are afraid of repeated failure or hurt, and have backed away from the will of God, then you need to transform and renew your mind! Allow your mind to be converted by God's

Word. The "power of Jesus' resurrection" has released all God's grace to us! Now we can overcome every hurt and failure from the past. We need to realize that nothing—no hurt, no wound, and no disappointment from our past—is greater than the power of Jesus within us!

Chapter 5

Make Me Whole!

Why do so many of the "saints of God" have "pity parties" even though they have been exposed to the very truth that can set them free? When they hear a preacher speak on a certain subject under the anointing of God, they go to him and say, "You just preached on something that has been bothering me all my life!" Then they go home feeling hopeless and despondent, and cry all week! Something is terribly wrong here.

God's Word is life, light, and truth. When you meet truth, you are supposed to be set free, not get discouraged! If God is our "all in all," and if we really understand that He is, then it should make a tremendous difference in our lives. Jesus told His disciples, "And ye shall know the truth, and the truth shall make you free" (Jn. 8:32). When He said they would *know* the truth, He meant they would *experience and exhibit* the truth. We are to be "doers of the word, and not hearers only" (Jas. 1:22)! Just what is this "truth" that sets us free? The truth is a person, Jesus Christ, the Son of God. When He dwells within us, His Spirit, His Word, and His will permeate our lives and drive out every unclean thing—if we yield to His gentle touch.

Learn Leah's Secret

Leah, the first wife of Jacob, developed the kind of attitude that brought healing from the bondage and bitterness created by her wounds of rejection. How did she do it? What was her secret? The answer could transform your life!

According to Genesis 29, Leah's father, Laban, tricked Jacob into marrying her. Jacob had worked for Laban for seven years with the agreement that his "wage" would be Laban's younger and prettier daughter, Rachel. When Jacob woke up the morning after his wedding feast, he discovered he had been given Leah instead—obviously their marriage got off to a bad start right from the beginning!

Leah knew that she wasn't wanted or loved, and she craved the affection of her husband. She knew Jacob thought she was homely compared to Rachel (she had "weak eyes," which might mean they were crossed). She thought, "If I have children for him, maybe he will feel differently about me." She had given Jacob the place in her heart that rightly belonged to God, thinking that Jacob's love would be her ultimate fulfillment and joy.

God Knew Leah Was Hated

The Bible says, "And when the Lord saw that Leah was hated, He opened her womb…" (Gen. 29:31). She gave birth to Reuben and said, "Surely the Lord hath looked upon my affliction; now therefore my husband will love me" (Gen. 29:32b). Yet Jacob's heart still did not change. Leah bore him a second son, and expressed her feelings in his name, Simeon, which means "unloved." Her third was named Levi, or "attached," revealing Leah's fresh hope that his birth would make the difference in Jacob's feelings for her, but to no avail.

Then the Scriptures tell us that Leah "conceived again, and bare a son: and she said, *Now will I praise the Lord*: therefore she called his name Judah [*praise*]; and left bearing" (Gen. 29:35). A dramatic change had occurred in Leah's life and in her attitude: She had reached the point we must all come to! Leah had realized that she had to stop giving birth to things that were "unfruitful." In other words, she was putting her hope in things that were not bringing about the desired effect.

All of Leah's childbearing efforts were "fruitless" *as far as her relationship with her husband was concerned*, since he had not changed. She stopped giving birth to attitudes that only added more wounds and hurts because she realized that those things were not helping her. They were not bringing wholeness or victory. We too must come to the place where we are willing to stop doing the same old things that get us nowhere and only result in more wounds.

When Leah gave birth to Judah, she stopped bearing children. *She stopped trying to reach wholeness and fulfillment through natural means.* Instead, she began to praise God! She had found her "portion" (or *inheritance*) in *Judah*—in *praise*! She had finally found the thing she really needed.

She Praised Herself to Freedom

The answer to Leah's need wasn't to be found locked up in a relationship with a man. She discovered her answer in praise when she put her trust in God and gave Him first place. She yielded the throne of her heart to Him and began to give Him the adoration and trust she had previously reserved for a man. That was the moment she began to walk in freedom!

In Genesis 49, Jacob decreed a prophetic blessing over his son Judah that said, in part: "The sceptre shall not depart from Judah..." (Gen. 49:10). The *sceptre* is symbolic of smiting the enemy and of ruling. Jesus Himself came from the line of Judah, and He holds all power and ultimate authority as the King of kings and Lord of lords. This verse reveals a vital truth: It is through *praise* that we can stand in the power and authority of God Most High! As we praise God, we will always "smite the enemy" and be victorious over his plans to destroy our lives!

Once we understand the power of praise and begin to walk in continual praise to God, we will no longer be subject to the evil plans of our enemy! We will have new power and authority to "step on the head of the enemy" (symbolic of triumph), and we will have complete victory! As we praise our God, we will literally walk right out of the frustrations and bitterness from our painful past! Right now, we can enter into a life of victorious wholeness as we sing and worship His holy name!

Believe, Receive, and Move!

We have learned that *God always presents truth for a purpose!* He expects us to *believe* it, *receive* it, and *move forward.* This principle was revealed early in the life and ministry of Moses, when he and the children of Israel were trapped between the Red Sea and Pharaoh's pursuing army in Exodus 14. You may be facing impossible circumstances today with no apparent escape, much as they were. It appeared that God had directed Moses to lead the children of Israel right into a bloody disaster! Everyone in that massive crowd of exiles knew the truth: They were in big trouble!

God brings every one of us to a place where we must acknowledge our problems! In our crises, we are forced to hear questions such as: "Why are you where you are? Why are you doing the things you are doing? And why are you acting in ways that continually bring you down?" God is saying to us, as He said to Israel, "Recognize your problem—you have come to the end of your own strength, your own answers, and your own means of escape!" We should be thankful that He never stops there! No, He brings us face to face with the problem, and then He presents the truth that will set us free.

The Lord doesn't show us our problems so we can build a permanent camp there! Nothing is accomplished when we are content to say, "Oh! Now I know why I am like this. Now I know what makes me tick." God says, "Now that you know the truth, *do something about it!*" Don't stop to write a book about "facing the problem"; go ahead and move out of that area of defeat!

Dancing and Singing

God told Israel through Moses: "...Fear ye not, stand still, and see the salvation of the Lord, which He will shew to you to day: for the Egyptians [symbolic of sin and backsliding] whom ye have seen to day, ye shall see them again no more for ever" (Ex. 14:13). God fulfilled His promise and delivered them, and the children of Israel crossed the Red Sea into freedom praising God, dancing, and singing "the song of Moses" unto the Lord (see Ex. 15:1-21).

The nation of Egypt and Pharaoh's rule in these passages symbolize our past sin, our desire to return to sin, and our compulsive meditation on the wounds of the past. As we trust and praise God, our wounds and hurts will become things of the past—we won't see them rule over us anymore. God brings us to a crisis where we must recognize them *so we can get rid of them forever*!

If you had not grown up with a father's warm, nurturing love and protection, then many of your problems may have stemmed from your lack. Now that you understand that truth, God wants to show how to climb up into "Father-God's" lap so He can bring peace and wholeness to your life. Armed with this truth, you can lay plans to become a "father" (an example and mentor) to other fatherless "children" in the family of God! You won't have to go back to the "Egypt" of past hurts, wounds, and slavery to sin because you have seen the truth. God will fight for you—while you hold your peace and behold His glory—just as He fought for Israel on that day long ago! (See Exodus 14:13-14.)

The Root Word Is "Act"

Now that God has revealed the root of your problems, you must *act* on that knowledge in God's way and God's time, not your own. If you have learned that many of your problems came from bad parental relationships, that does not give you the right to confront your daddy or mother in anger! There is a godly way to confront your pain that always brings healing and reconciliation.

Don't tell your father, "You are a rotten scoundrel. I know why I am going through this—I don't even know how to be a father to my children because you were never there for me!" Don't tell your mother, "I am a terrible wife today because of your rotten example, Mother. It is your fault that I am ruining my life, and my children's lives too!" That is not the way to be whole. The Lord says, "I shall fight for you, *and you shall hold your peace*." When you *know* the truth that He really is your El Shaddai, then you can "hold your peace" and allow Him to deal with all the issues and relationships of the past. It is a new day. He has given you a new start!

Apparently Moses did what most of us have done too. Even though he had heard the promises of God and faced the truth, he evidently still "cried out to God" because the Lord asked him, "...Wherefore criest thou unto Me? speak unto the children of Israel, *that they go forward*" (Ex. 14:15). God is saying to us today, "Why are you still crying? I have given you the message to *go forward!*"

Stop Remembering When

We cannot receive God's promise of wholeness and victory as long as we *live in the past*. We need to stop "remembering when." Our children are helpless to grow and develop healthy emotional lives as long as the adults in their lives still "play with the toy trucks and cars" of their past. It is time to emerge from childhood and recognize the truth—and begin to walk in it.

Every local church seems to have a few people who refuse to grow up and move beyond the hurts of their childhood. They often weaken the Body because they are always "remembering" how other churches, pastors, and Christians hurt them in the past. They rehearse all their hurts at the "other church" every time their current pastor tries to disciple them or bring them into a knowledge of the truth. Don't be like the children of Reuben and Gad, who discouraged the other Israelites from moving forward (see Num. 32:1-7). God wants us to let go of the past and *move forward* in Him.

God told Moses, "But lift thou up thy rod, and stretch out thine hand over the sea..." (Ex. 14:16). The *rod* of Moses represented the *authority* God gave him to lead His people. Since Moses was tending sheep when God appeared to him, the rod was most likely a shepherd's crook. One end was always used as a weapon to *protect* the sheep, and the other end was used to *correct* the sheep.

The Rod of Selection and Correction

It is the same in the Church today: One part of the shepherd's rod (anointed authority of leadership) is used to pull the people out of danger (mercy), while the other end is used for correction (judgment). Ancient shepherds had to wound the legs of those sheep that were always leaping outside of their protective folds (just like modern "church-hoppers"). If the shepherd doesn't recognize and correct this harmful behavior, these wandering sheep will quickly fall prey to predator wolves, starve to death, or fall into a snare or dangerous crevice.

Although God has placed shepherds over His sheep in the Body of Christ, He has also given every believer a "rod of authority" to part the seas blocking progress in their own lives. Jesus said, "Behold, I give unto you power [authority]...over all the power of the enemy..." (Lk. 10:19). God declared, "No weapon that is formed [or devised] against thee shall prosper; and every tongue that shall rise against thee in judgment thou shalt condemn..."

(Is. 54:17). God says, "Pick up the rod. Pick up the authority I have given you. Stretch out your hand!"

God didn't tell Moses to just pick up his rod and "keep it in a safe place" under the bed. He said, "Stretch out thine hand..." (Ex. 14:16). The *hands* are symbolic of service, work, ministry, and worship. He has promised to bless you "in all that thou settest thine hand unto" (Deut. 28:8). He is telling us, "Stretch out your hand over the barriers that hold you back and hinder you!" We can never go forward into wholeness in God's promises unless we know and exercise the authority we have been given. It is time to part the barriers and "go through"!

The Only Way "To" Is "Through"

The things that block the way to our "promised land" have got to go! There is no other way around problems! Only the roots of our problems lie behind us in the past. God used the Red Sea to separate and divide Israel from their slavery in Egypt and launch them toward a new future in the Promised Land. What is He using your "Red Sea" for? He is separating you from the sin, bondage, pain, and even the comforts of your life before Christ! He is bringing you face to face with a seemingly immovable obstacle so you will know that He, and He *alone*, is your Deliverer.

Throughout the Old and New Testaments, God used the precious ointment of *myrrh* to represent His desire to heal our *bitterness*. Myrrh represents God's divine intention to turn every painful situation of our lives into places where His sweetness can be released. It was one of the key ingredients used to prepare the anointing oil used in the tabernacle and temple ceremonies of consecration and worship (see Ex. 30:23). Myrrh was also prized as a perfume or fragrance, but it had a bitter taste when it was crushed!

Myrrh symbolizes the way our Savior suffered until He died—all to bring us eternal life. Myrrh was used for many things. Besides being used for making the anointing oil for religious ceremonies, it was also part of a potent painkiller, and was a key ingredient in the embalming process in the ancient world.

The Myrrh That Makes Us Better

God's precious anointing destroys every yoke (see Is. 10:27). His anointing (symbolized by myrrh) is His divine provision for everything we will ever go through! However, we must stand in the authority of the anointing that He has given us in Christ. An inescapable part of the healing and deliverance process is His revelation of the bitterness in our past. The truth that He is our "all in all" destroys the lie that says we must stay in the miserable shape we are in! He isn't out to devastate us or make us depressed. He only reveals the truth to make us better.

When the wise men brought the myrrh to the Christ-child in Matthew 2:11, they were, in essence, prophetically demonstrating that He would "suffer unto death" for all mankind. In Song of Solomon 1:13 Jesus, *our Beloved,* is described as a "bundle of myrrh...betwixt my breasts." The breast is seen as the "place of affection," and the Beloved is the sweet-smelling "painkiller" who soothes and heals all the hurt of our emotions and affections. Jesus Christ will remove the pain from the situations of your past and ease your heart as you go through your valley today.

Jesus Needed No Myrrh

The Jews used myrrh in an attempt to "sweeten the wounds" of the dead when preparing a body for burial (see Jn. 19:39). Myrrh was used on the body of Jesus after His bitter death on the cross, *but He didn't really need it*—He wasn't going to be staying in that grave! Many of us have been wounded and "pierced" from early childhood, and people have tried to "sweeten up" those places. Ever since resurrection morning, Christians have been able to say, "I don't need this myrrh anymore; I am going to come out of this 'death' too! You don't need to embalm me because I plan to rise from this place of death. I am going to let my life and attitudes and words demonstrate the resurrection power of God Almighty!"

Jesus took all bitterness of sin, death, and sickness on Himself at Calvary so we wouldn't have to receive it (see Jn. 19:29-30). When He said, "It is finished," the last claim of bitterness on our lives was destroyed! He took all the torment of bitterness on Himself that day in order that we could be free of its crippling effects. He set us free to love those who try to sow the seed of bitterness anew in our lives and minds. Jesus was offered myrrh mixed with wine (see Mk. 15:23), but He refused to receive anything that would lessen the pain. He hung on that cross to become our divine myrrh, our eternal painkiller Himself. He took the pain so we wouldn't have to endure it.

Jesus Still Heals!

Jesus is the myrrh, the perfume, the anointing oil, and the divine painkiller for the Church. He can heal your hurt and wounded emotions, and kill the pain caused by heartbreak, rejection, disappointment, abandonment, and other devastations of your mind and heart. He alone can—and will—forever heal the hurts that have damaged your mind or emotions. He has the power to heal the pain of abuses that destroyed your private and personal feelings of security and safety, and distorted your views of romance and love.

It all comes down to one all-important question: *Wilt thou be made whole?* Do you really want to be whole and free? Are you willing to follow the Great Physician's orders to be cured? You must lay aside every excuse. He will ask you to release every memory from the past and forgive every offense from the present. Healing begins as you lay aside every garment you have used to hide the "real you" inside—"casting all your care upon Him; for He careth for you" (1 Pet. 5:7)!

Chapter 6

God Mixes the Bitter With the Sweet

No matter how powerful we think we have become, we must obey God when He calls us. He had a message for influential Jeremiah. God told the mighty prophet of Israel, "Come down to the potter's house. Don't sit there in your house, but come to the potter's place, where you can get fixed" (see Jer. 18).

The Master Potter wants to put your shattered life back together, but healing only comes when you are willing to get on the potter's wheel! There are times on that wheel when we feel like we are just going around and around in circles, getting nowhere fast!

The truth is that all the while, He is mending and reshaping us. Sometimes we have to keep going around on the wheel longer than other people, or longer than we think is "necessary." When this happens, it is probably because the Master Potter knows there are still some cracks and weaknesses in the clay of our character. He is determined to remove those things so they won't destroy us when pressures come.

Finally "Fit for Use"

If we will patiently endure the working of the Potter's skillful hands, then when He is finished, we won't even be able to tell where the cracks and mars were! We will no longer see the hurts and wounds. Instead, we will be the complete vessels He planned for us to be, and we will finally be "fit for the Master's use" because we were *willing* to allow Him to do the work.

Some of us come to the wheel of God terribly fragmented, but the Master Potter wants to put our lives back together again. Some of us are fragmented in our minds; some are fragmented in spirit. Half of us are bound up in hurts from the past with our daddies, while others of us are stuck back in ancient Egypt with our wounded memories of Mother. Some of us are lingering in the graveyard, and others of us are hopelessly chained to old relationships. God is saying to each of us: "I want to put you back together again! Let Me bring all the fragmented parts of your life together into wholeness. I am your Creator. I can recreate what has been destroyed, if you will just trust Me and let Me have your hurts."

God cannot do anything for us if we are not willing to let Him, for He will never force us against our will. Sometimes we keep walking around in our wretched state because we secretly enjoy it! Many born-again, Spirit-filled Christians who have heard the Word of God, and know He provided for their healing and deliverance from bitterness and unforgiveness, continue to walk around in the same miserable state they had *before* they met Christ!

Was God unable to deliver them? Absolutely not! They remain there because they want to be there. Perhaps they are enjoying the pity and attention they get from others!

Beware of Willful Wallowing

Do you fit this description? Then be warned! Be very careful that you don't destroy other soldiers while you willfully wallow in your past. Don't make negative or disparaging statements about your church, your pastor, or any other Christians in the Body. "Oh, I've been with them for more than 12 years, but then, nobody really loves me or cares about me here." God hates those who "[sow] discord among brethren" (Prov. 6:19). Don't discourage anyone from seeking the godly nurture and love he needs to start back on the road of recovery.

As we cry out for deliverance and healing from the hurts of our past, God will *bring us "into the suffering" to "deliver us from the suffering."* God brought Israel to the bitter waters of Marah to quench their thirst in the desert. He allows bitter circumstances and relationships to come along so we can learn how to be delivered from them and overcome them. While the children of Israel were in Egypt under the cruel bondage of slavery, they ate bitter herbs. In the bondage of our past, we also have eaten "bitterness."

Turned From Bitter to Sweet

After a three-day journey into the desert and away from the land of their bondage, the children of Israel finally found some water. When they tasted the water of the spring, it was so bitter that they called the place *Marah*, which means "bitter." Moses cried out to God on behalf of the people, "...and the Lord shewed him a tree, which when he had cast into the waters, the waters were made sweet" (Ex. 15:25a). Another tree on Calvary was cast on the bitter waters of our sin, and the root of David, Jesus Christ, paid the price to sweeten our bitter hearts. On that third day, we too received the healing power of God to overcome every bitter situation in our lives—whether past or present! The Lover of our souls issued an eternal declaration to our race: "I can turn your bitter situations into sweet situations—if you will trust Me!"

One of the clearest examples of the role of bitterness in our wholeness is revealed in Proverbs 20:30, which says, "The blueness of a wound cleanseth away evil [infection]: so do stripes the inward parts of the belly." The Bible says, "For whom the Lord loveth He chasteneth, and scourgeth every son whom He receiveth" (Heb. 12:6). He disciplines us and trains us so we can be healed and become fruitful. Chastisement and correction cleanse away evil. The Lord is dealing with many in the Body of Christ today who have not been willing to let Him "cleanse away the evil." They want to struggle along, doing things the wrong way. Then they wonder why "their way" leaves them in such a mess!

Heal From the Inside Out

If you still have the root of a problem in your heart, God will put you in the same type of situation again to get you delivered and heal you! He will make sure you confront it so it can be dealt with. The former prostitute who is bothered every time someone talks about prostitution is not delivered. There is a scab over the sore, but the wound within is not healed yet. You have experienced true healing from the inside out when you can talk about a past problem or experience all night long, and not be bothered or feel guilty over it.

Years ago, I (Vernette) greeted a lady in the church with a big hug, and she said, "Oh no, they will think we are lesbians!" I said, "Honey, they might think you are, but they sure won't think I am!" That woman had a "scab" covering a wound that was still sore. Whether the preacher is talking about lazy wives, adulterous husbands, or rebellious women, you won't be bothered if you are really whole in those areas. You shouldn't start fidgeting when the pastor starts talking about gossiping—if you know you don't gossip! What are you worried about, if you are really delivered?

You are really healed from a problem when you can respond calmly to someone who says, "I think you have this problem." You can look them in the eye without getting upset, and tell them, "Oh no, you can't be talking about me. I'm free! I am healed and I know it, for God has delivered me." However, when you are still bound and the wound still hurts, nearly anything at all can make you angry and upset.

Is God "Preaching Your Secrets"?

Many times during services God pinpoints a person who is hiding his hurts behind a facade of healing. That person nearly always get upset because "that minister stood right in front of me and preached my secrets." Usually the Lord doesn't let the minister know who the person is. People often come up to us after a sermon or prophetic ministry and say, "You preached all my business! Why didn't you just speak to me privately? You didn't have to expose it to the whole church!"

Most of the time we didn't even know their identity until the people opened their mouth! We just have to tell them, "We weren't even thinking about you; God didn't reveal who He was speaking about. If you hadn't said something just now, we still wouldn't know!"

God has a divine purpose for each of us, and sometimes that purpose includes hardship and persecution. Pilate was willing to release Jesus, but the crowd shouted, "Crucify Him! Crucify Him!" (see Lk. 23:21) Death on the cross was part of the divine purpose for our Savior's life; it was predestined by God. The reason Jesus Christ came to earth was to suffer crucifixion. The Bible assures us, "Yea, and all that will live godly in Christ Jesus shall [will!] suffer persecution" (2 Tim. 3:12).

If you are living for God and pressing into Him, should you get upset when you go through persecution? God said, "Many are the afflictions of the righteous: but the Lord delivereth him out of them all" (Ps. 34:19). Afflictions, or trials, and persecution are signs that you are living a godly life. Those who live "half-mast" try to straddle the fence—half in, half out of God's holy Kingdom. Satan doesn't have to worry about them. He knows *they* are no danger to him!

Climb on Your "Own" Cross

Crucifixion is supposed to be a "solo act," but many of us insist on "crucifying" everyone around us when we experience a trial! We make our poor spouses miserable by our efforts to *nail them up on the same tree* with us! Never mind that God may not be dealing with them in the same areas! Some of us are happy to try to hammer those nails in them too, while we think, "If I have to be on this cross, then I'm going to make sure someone else is up there with me!"

Jesus approached the cross with a different perspective. He had already been sentenced and was hanging on the cross, yet those around Him were still taunting Him, shouting out mocking statements like, "Physician, heal Yourself and we'll believe! If You are so powerful, then call legions of angels to deliver You! You must not be who You said You were—God has gone off and forgotten You!" (See Matthew 27:39-44.) One of the two thieves crucified with Jesus had the good sense to break from the rest of the mockers. He said, "...we receive the due reward of our deeds: but this man hath done nothing amiss" (Lk. 23:41).

Jesus did nothing wrong, yet He endured all that suffering for us. Jesus suffered daily in some way. In a sense, He went to the "Gethsemane" of agony on a daily basis. Gethsemane represents "dying to self," and in the last stages of His ministry, Jesus had to pray continually until He was able to say, "Not My will, but Thine, be done" (Lk. 22:42).

"Thy Will" Kills My Will

Sometimes the hardest thing we have to say in this life is: "Thy will!" We say, "Now Lord, of course You *could* do it Your way, but how about adding this to it? And just don't let anyone correct me, Lord. Don't let me have to be rebuked, okay? Don't ever let me get hurt." We build defensive "walls" on top of our false presumptions of "what we think God should do." The reality of it all is that when life's storms batter those presumptuous walls and self-made plans, we are either severely damaged or we fall apart completely (see Ezek. 13:1-11).

God can bring us through and make us strong if we will allow our hurts to become stepping-stones to victory in our lives. When we say, "I won't ever reach out again. I have to protect myself, Lord, so don't even try to reach in or get close to me," we shut out every healing messenger God sends us! We must tear down those walls by allowing the Holy Spirit to guide us to the truth that will make us free.

We need to face the facts: We all need to love and receive love! It is worth the risk of being hurt again. Sometimes life seems to let us "love and get hurt" only to "love and get hurt again"! How many times have we hurt Jesus Christ? We want to withdraw and run from the risk of pain when others hurt us, but when we disobey or hurt Jesus, we turn around and get right in His face again! Jesus taught us how to forgive instantly, even in His agony and pain suspended on the cross between the brass heavens and the mocking earth! He looked into His tormentors' taunting faces through swollen eyes and said, "Father, forgive them; for they know not what they do" (Lk. 23:34)! At the end, He commended Himself into the Father's hands. Jesus wants to teach us how to do the same by His grace. He wants to teach us how to rest in God, forgive in the face of affliction and hurt, and put ourselves in the arms of our loving Father-God.

We Never Walk Alone

Sometimes we think God has deserted us, but Jesus promised to never forsake us (see Heb. 13:5). When Jesus took all our sin upon Himself on the cross, God the Righteous One turned His face from the filth that obscured His Son. In that agonizing moment, for the first time since the birth of time, Jesus said, "Father, why have You forsaken Me?" (see Mt. 27:46) Jesus bore the devastation of separation from communion with His Father so we would never have to endure separation from our God (unless we choose to walk away from Him).

Jesus took all our bitterness so we wouldn't have to carry it. He took the bitterness that was offered to Him on a sponge, but He refused the painkiller because He understood that He must bear all our pains. We can cast all of them on Him and trust Him to bring the balm of healing to our wounded, shattered lives...*if we only will*!

He refused the painkiller of mingled wine and myrrh because He knew that if He refused the pain, we would have to find another remedy. He also knew some would refuse what He had done in taking our pain, and that they would try to find another remedy. Yet He bore it all on Calvary anyway, and He is the only One qualified to heal the hurts and take out all the pain. He can help you to give up the pain you thought you could never give up!

Jesus Forgives

Jesus forgave the very people who slandered and whispered against Him. He forgave the jealous religious leaders who had conspired to see Him destroyed. Even in the midst of the modern Church, many look and say, "They're always preaching and testifying about God's power, so why are they sick?" or "If they can see so much in the Spirit, then why didn't they see that person who was plotting to hurt them? If they are so knowledgeable, why didn't they see that betrayal or problem coming?"

Any time a person begins to minister publicly in the gifts of the Spirit, people are bound to whisper, judge, and slander. When the gift is prophetic, or the word of wisdom or knowledge manifests, many people expect the minister to "see everything." (That's not even scriptural! See Second Kings 4:8-27.) Even ministers who operate powerfully in certain areas will also have their times of testing and trial! The most important thing is for each of us to trust the goodness and mercy of God in every trial. He has called us to forgive those who hurt us, and to keep our attitudes sweet and loving. In the midst of a trial, God will tell you to bear it, and He will help you do it.

Betrayal Breeds Compassion

The Lord knew Judas would betray Him, yet He treated Judas the same way He treated the rest of the disciples. Jesus knew that without Judas, He could never fulfill His destiny! Each one of us "needs" a "Judas." (If Jesus had one, we probably need several!) Each of us must pass the test of having someone be close to us, and then betray and forsake us. It is the greatest test of true compassion. If you don't have compassion for others, nothing will develop that characteristic of loving understanding and patience in you like *betrayal*! Remember, it doesn't mean there is "something wrong with you"; Jesus was betrayed too.

Those who are closest to you are often those who hurt you the most. Afterward, they are usually in for a surprise! Lucifer didn't realize that the reason he looked so good was because the unequalled glory of God was shining on him! In the same way, some people in the Church don't realize that they "look good" because God allowed them to stand with genuinely good people! They don't realize that their gift is "sharp" because God placed them under the "umbrella" or spiritual covering of another minister with an even stronger and more seasoned anointing.

Some people may begin to think that they can "see higher" and "preach better" than their God-given mentors. They unknowingly (or sometimes, purposely) follow in the footsteps of David's eldest son, Absalom, and take a strategic position at the "gate" (the entrance to the sanctuary). There they lay the groundwork to steal the hearts of sheep with their tongues (see 2 Sam. 15:2)! They will say things like, "If *I were pastor,* I could do this better," or "I think it's time I *stepped in and fixed things* on my own. You really need someone who *better understands* your needs..."

Rebellion Is Dangerous

Other people with a little more maturity may simply say, "I think I am ready to be an independent minister, out on my own." (Now, if your spiritual covering agrees that you are mature enough to handle independent ministry, well and good; but if they don't agree, and you rebel, then you have opened yourself to the enemy's wiles.) Lucifer "lost his place" in Heaven, was stripped of the anointing of Heaven's "praise and worship leader," and was cast out of God's presence because of these same attitudes and ulterior motives (see Is. 14:12). Rebellion is always a dangerous thing. If you truly have a gift and calling, then the same God who gave them to you is fully able to move you into full-time service—in His timing. In the meantime, be patient and wait on the Lord, doing with diligence all that He gives you to do in your local church.

God knew about lucifer's defection and Judas' betrayal *before* they took place. Why didn't He do something about it? God's purposes are always "multi-layered." He knew that these betrayals would be examples showing us how to handle the betrayals and problems we would experience. He knew that we needed the *truth* of His word to strengthen us. Normally, you are hurt most deeply by the people you "hang out" with the most, by the people you pray for the most, and those you help financially. God requires us *not* to retaliate, but to freely forgive and love them, for He forgives us as we forgive others (see Mt. 6:12).

Crushed Bitterness Is Fragrant

We become mature through forgiveness, not bitterness. However, in order for us to be made whole, there had to be some bitterness (crushed myrrh) to make the anointing oil to destroy our yoke. God allows some bitterness to be mixed with the sweet in our lives. In fact, the anointing oil required twice as much bitterness (myrrh) as any of the other spices (see Ex. 30:22-25)! When "bitter" situations are mixed with the "sweet" (God's grace), a holy anointing pours out of our lives and becomes a fragrant offering to God!

If we simply coast through easy circumstances and "sweet" situations in our lives, we will become passive, weak, and cowardly Christians who will buckle under any hardship or confrontation! People who are used to hard physical labor quickly discover their strengths and weaknesses. They develop callouses where blisters used to form. They suffer more cuts, nicks, and injuries than other people, but they know how to treat them, and they also tend to heal quickly. Through hard experience, they become confident in their abilities and physical stamina. The Bible talks about believers "who by reason of use [lots of practice] have their senses exercised [trained] to discern both good and evil" (Heb. 5:14). The truth is that we need the rough times and the hard roads to help us grow and mature.

We need the challenge of tests and trials to continually remind us to let Jesus, our "painkiller," touch our hearts and emotions, keeping us soft and pliable in His hands. We won't learn this truth unless we are willing to go through difficult times with trust in our hearts and praise on our lips! God will test us and test us again until our response is one that brings glory to God.

After Failure: Stand and Help

Jesus told Peter in advance, "When you are converted, when you turn back to Me again, strengthen your brothers" (see Lk. 22:32). He didn't say Peter would strengthen the other disciples *while* he was going through the trial (and failure), but *after* he had come through it! Some of us can't help anyone else because we are still dragging our spiritual feet! We haven't come through the fire ourselves yet. We're still waiting for someone else to come back and help us.

Once you've been through something and come out victorious on the other side, then you can help somebody else who is struggling with a trial. There are a lot of people who are full of advice with no experience to back it up, but Paul the scarred apostle wrote, "For the kingdom of God is not in word, but in *power*" (1 Cor. 4:20). Once you have gone through a difficult trial and passed through it, you will discover a new anointing flowing through your life to help others be free from the yoke of their bondage!

The Lord will sometimes allow situations to occur that help us see the harmful or evil things still buried deep in our hearts. God allows us to know what is in us so we will acknowledge it and work on getting it right. The Holy Spirit is the Revealer who constantly works in your heart to reveal areas where you still need help to win total victory. If you say, "Oh, well, I never curse," then the Lord may allow someone to enter your life who could "aggravate a curse out of a corpse"! You can't get freed or healed of something by running or trying to hide from it. God's way (the *right* way) is to confront it, deal with it, and then go forward.

"I Have Prayed for Thee"

Sometimes the truth really hurts. When Peter denied Christ, he heard the rooster crow and he *remembered* what Jesus had said. Jesus had foretold Peter's betrayal, but He had also prophesied that Peter would *come through* and follow Him again. *The Lord's prophetic word and intercessory prayer brought Peter through!* Jesus said, "But I have prayed for thee, that thy faith fail not..." (Lk. 22:32). Jesus knew that when the truth hit Peter, he would feel so low that he would want to give up, for he *didn't know that failure was in his heart*! God always knows what is in our hearts, and He is always prepared to bring us through, giving us divine encouragement and strength as we go.

Perhaps Peter was quick and bold to proclaim what he would "never do" because Jesus was standing right next to him. His life was not on the line that night; his faith had not been challenged to the level it soon would be! What do you do when your faith is challenged? Do you love and forgive, even in the face of hurt and betrayal?

Peter did not know what was in his heart. Jesus had to stop him from cutting people up "in His name" in Matthew 26:51-52! Some of us are "killing people" with the Word, and "cutting off ears" in the name of helping Jesus. Some well-meaning and sincere people are "zealous without knowledge," and they are bringing reproach on the Kingdom because their actions don't demonstrate the love of Jesus. You may be sincere, but your actions will be "sincerely wrong" if they are hurting or destroying people in the name of "helping" them or the Lord.

Out of the Abundance

Peter was warming himself by the fire in the high priest's courtyard when something deep in his heart was revealed. Afraid for his life, Peter began cursing and denying that he even knew Jesus! Cursing is a sign that you "don't know Him." A hidden thing in Peter's heart had slipped out—it can't come out if it's not in there. The Bible says, "For out of the abundance of the heart the mouth speaketh" (Mt. 12:34b). Sometimes God provides situations to help root out the things hidden deep in our hearts that we need to recognize and deal with.

Have you noticed that Jesus didn't get bitter toward Peter when he denied Him? How will you react when you are going through the worst thing you will ever go through, when you are being "crucified" by the vicious slanders of others, when you are being persecuted and false accusations are flying from all directions? What would you think if your closest friend, the one you are always with, the friend you just knew would stand by you and stick up for you—sneaks off during your biggest crisis? What if he told everyone, "I don't know him either."

When we begin to know *something* of what Jesus went through, it is then that His character of compassion and loving forgiveness is developed in us. Peter received a great deal of Jesus' time, and he was specially groomed to help lead the Jerusalem church. He was one of the three disciples on the Mount of Transfiguration with Jesus; he was the spokesman for all the disciples. If anyone was going to stick with Jesus and not betray Him, it would have been Peter, the bold and brave disciple!

One Man Followed

But wait! There was one man who didn't leave the Lord...he followed Him right into the inner court of the high priest! John hadn't been promised that he would get to lead the Church. John wasn't the one who would preach that anointed sermon on the Day of Pentecost and lead thousands to Christ. John came out of the inner court and led Peter in, possibly because he thought Peter would be a support for the Lord in His hour of need. When Peter denied Jesus, John could have said, "See, I knew You couldn't trust that loud-mouthed boaster, Lord! You should have let *me* be the leader and preacher! See, Jesus, I am the only one here who is *really* on Your side." Instead, John was content with his place in Jesus' affections. He didn't try to take the place of another, and he didn't get bitter because Peter played a more prominent role in the Church than he.

Only God Makes the Assignments

John knew that God sovereignly places people in certain positions and anointings in the Body by appointment. The Church is *not* built on a "buddy system" where everyone has to "share and share alike." The gifts and anointings of God don't have anything to do with who our closest friend is, or who our parents are. It has nothing to do with position or natural relationships. Those who are around people who operate in the gifts of the Spirit will learn how the Spirit operates, and will often be more confident and bold in stepping out to minister, but the "giving of the gift" has nothing to do with man or man's whims—it is God's business. God may not choose you for a particular position, gift, or ministry—even if you yearn for it or beg Him for it. That doesn't mean He doesn't love you; it simply means God has a different assignment for you.

It is time to stop mourning over what is *not* ours, and get up and go forward! Israel went around and around in the wilderness for 40 years because people moaned over what they *didn't have,* and were too afraid to reach out for what they *should have had.* In the end, the entire generation died out there in the wilderness. Only Joshua and Caleb were confident of God and His ability to bring them through. They declared, "We are well able to come over and take the land!" They alone were allowed to enter the Promised Land. God is looking for people in His Church today who will say, "We are well able!"

Chapter 7

You Can Make It

No matter what failure, frustration, or problem you face, it is not too difficult for God! Nothing can come against you that is greater than the power, love, and grace of God. John the apostle declared, "Ye are of God, little children, and have overcome them: because greater is He that is in you, than he that is in the world" (1 Jn. 4:4). The Bible says, "Jesus Christ the same yesterday, and to day, and for ever" (Heb. 13:8)! Only God can step back into your "yesterday," and He can make your "today" all right. Only He can go into your tomorrow and prepare the way! There is nothing that could possibly happen that is greater than the power of the God who dwells within you!

Don't let the frustrations of life stop you from being all God wants you to be. Perhaps you have caught yourself sitting in a church service listening to someone preach or teach God's Word, but though you heard the message, *you weren't able to receive it* because you were thinking *frustrated thoughts* about what is not working at home or on your job.

I Won't Stop!

Too often we let problems frustrate us, delay us, and slow down our walk with God, when they should be helping us grow in our faith! Every problem and trial should teach you to stand up and say, "Wait a minute—I'm not going to let this hinder me or bog me down! I will not let this stop me from praising the Lord!" We need to look at our troubles and declare, " 'Greater is He that is in me than he that is in the world!' I can't stop, and I won't stop!"

Sometimes we look at our problems and think, "Nothing ever works out for me! Nobody ever seems to care for me. It's always that way—failure and rejection seem to follow me around." If we're not careful, that frustration can lead to anger and bitterness. In the natural sense, your bitterness might seem justified because people really have hurt you. But the God in you is greater than those hurts. Why try to find a reason to be bitter when, if you'll release it all to God, His power will heal you and restore your joy!

Do you remember our discussion of frustration? It brings you to nothing, and it discourages you from making an effort or trying again. Does that describe you? God says you can be fulfilled! God says you can rise again! God says you can do all things through Christ who strengthens you (see Phil. 4:13)!

Hold On to Your Spouse

There are many people who are so frustrated in their marriage that they won't even try anymore. All they talk about is divorce. "I'll just get rid of him (or her)—he never does what I want. I think I'll just get somebody else!" We have one question for you if you have been contemplating divorce: "What if no one else wants you?" There are many more women than there are men in the United States. If you have a husband, maybe you had better hold on to him! Studies have shown there are at least seven other women waiting for yours to be "turned loose"!

Some married people complain about what their spouses won't let them do, and what they won't let them have. Meanwhile, lonely single people (of course they're not *all* lonely or eyeing your spouse) are saying, "I can't believe you want to leave them because they don't hang their clothes up, or let you get your 60-dollar hairdo!" Some single ladies would tell dissatisfied wives, "Girl, if I just had one man who would let me have his name, then *I* would buy the corn flakes! I'd pick up his clothes for a lifetime just to have a good man beside me!" Some of us are complaining, sowing seeds of bitterness, and destroying our relationships with our words *because we've forgotten that it was the favor and goodness of God that let us be married in the first place*!

Another way we stop moving forward in our walk with God is by giving in to our fear of other people's opinions! Our society has bought many of the devil's lies and made them the social "norm." Unfortunately, nobody bothered to check with God about these so-called "norms." Men have to avoid certain things or natural emotions because they're afraid that if their "buddies" see them, they will say they're not "real men." (It seems like the best definition of a "real man" would come from the Creator of the first "real man.")

What Is a "Real Man"?

We really appreciate men who are so comfortable in their masculinity that they are not afraid to get up in church and get involved. If they are exceptionally secure, they might even do a mime, or a dance! Now men who are afraid of the disapproval of others, and insecure men without a real understanding of what it means to be "a real man," may look at "real men" and sneer and poke fun. Some men are so foolish that they think it is "sissy" for a man to be involved in church, or even to use verbs and adjectives correctly when they speak! (Perhaps they think the appearance of stupidity and ignorance is attractive or manly!)

Some men have little chance of being good husbands because they run around with "friends" who are dominating them with their crazed ideas *more* than the Word of God influences them. Some men in the Church run their household and marriage the way those "good ol' boys" tell them to, instead of God's way!

If you don't know who you are, you'll let others intimidate and stop you from doing what is right. They will even stop you from following God if you let them. Why? Your faithfulness to God will shame them. The Bible record is clear: "For as many as are led by the Spirit of God, they are the sons [and daughters] of God" (Rom. 8:14). Now that you are led by the Spirit, you don't need to be moved by other people's notions and views that are contrary to God's ways. If you spend your time listening to the critical views of others and trying to win their approval, then you won't do anything in this life!

No More Negatives!

People will always make snide comments about those who enjoy great freedom in public praise and worship to the Lord. They will even go so far as to declare that it isn't of God (conveniently overlooking the entire Book of Psalms, and most of the Epistles to the churches). In the past, we listened to the negative things people said and backed away from freely worshiping the Lord without inhibition. No more! We have made the decision to press on—no matter what men say about us. We decided to let them talk about us all they want—people talked about Jesus too! Was He wrong? No. He steadfastly continued to do the Father's will, and that is what we intend to do.

Did you know that there is a "satanic" representative assigned by satan to stop God's purpose for your life and family? It's true! The devil intends to frustrate you (to make you of "none effect," to discourage you so you won't ever try again). When Daniel prayed and fasted, God immediately heard his prayer and dispatched an angel to him. But the Scriptures tell us there was a satanic representative or prince over Persia (Daniel was a Hebrew captive living in Persia) who tried to stop or hinder God's answer to Daniel's prayer by withstanding the angelic messenger from God. After 21 days of conflict, God sent the mighty archangel Michael to assist the messenger angel, and God's answer was quickly delivered to Daniel (see Dan. 10:11-14).

Just Don't Give Up!

The enemy will come to your house and try to stop everything God intends to do in your life, but remember this: The Greater One in you has already promised you that "no weapon that is formed against thee shall prosper" (Is. 54:17). Satan and his imps cannot stop any person who will be determined like Daniel, who faithfully prayed and expected answers for 21 days without wavering. You need to keep after it like Abraham Lincoln, who just would not give up—no matter what other people said. You need to say, "If I miss it today, I'll get it tomorrow. If I fail this year, if I don't get this job, I won't stop. If the door is shut, I'll try another—that is not the only door in the world. If I fail a class, I will go back to school until I pass it and move on up!"

Many people in recent years flunked out of school when they were younger. If you are in that situation, the fact that you didn't graduate does *not* mean you are a dummy! You probably just couldn't "get things together" in your teen years. (That stage of human development has never been known for its wealth of great wisdom or discipline, in general.) Is there a dream that seemed to die when you failed to finish school?

Stay There Until You Get It!

Perhaps you have always wanted to be a beautician or a nurse; a lawyer or an accountant; or perhaps a certified diesel mechanic. It's not too late! Take an accurate measure of yourself: You have the help and guidance of the Holy Spirit now. You are older and wiser, and now you are confident that you can "get it together." At this point, that "satanic representative" will try to frustrate, delay, and defeat you. He doesn't want you to succeed or be what you were destined to be in Christ! Now is the time to be like Daniel. Set your mind to *understand* the purposes of God. Pray and believe, then you will receive your answer! When you pray, expect an answer and *stay there* until you get it. Stay right there until God breaks that demon loose so your answer can come.

When Jacob asked God to help him, and to deliver him from the hand of his brother Esau, at first it looked like the situation was getting worse (see Gen. 32:9–33:16)! You may be having hard times right now, *even though you have been praying.* You have decided you want to go on with God. You have reached the place where it does not matter what it takes—you want all God has for you. You will no longer allow the past or people's opinions to sway or hinder you. You have cried out to God, "Fix me! Make me, shape me, mold me, God! Help me be what You want me to be!" You made a good start, and then everything began to go wrong...

First you stepped into the will of God and under the anointing. You kept yourself around people who prayed in the power of the Holy Ghost; people whose commitment and prayers inspired and challenged you. When you heard them start praying, "Fix me, God!"; then you said, "Yeah, Lord!" When they cried out, "Make and shape me"; you said, "Hallelujah! Amen!" When they prayed, "Whatever it takes, God"; you shouted, "Amen!"

You Need an Identity Change

Just yesterday, you were sure you were standing at the threshold of promise and breakthrough, like Jacob at the river Jabbok in Genesis 32:22. Then everything started turning upside down. You shouldn't be surprised— *Jabbok* means "to empty out (self), to pour forth; to spread out (as a fruitful vine).[1] Just as Jacob had to wrestle all night long and not give up, so you will have to overcome and be persistent if you want to cross the river! It may not seem like it, but God is overcoming those hindrances you asked Him to take care of. He is out to *change your name and identity.*

Don't be surprised if some of your friends start acting funny and avoid talking to you—they don't recognize you anymore. Whatever is frustrating your progress, whatever is holding you back, God is moving things out, He's moving things in, and He's rearranging the other things in your life. He wants you to fulfill His marvelous plan for your life more than you do! He has heard your prayer, and He is moving obstacles out of the way for you.

Jacob prayed a life-changing prayer: "...Lord [You said] unto me, Return unto thy country, and to thy kindred, and I will deal well with thee" (Gen. 32:9). God had brought Jacob to the banks of the river Jabbok, where Jacob had to be willing to be emptied of self and all self-interest. Jacob had to be willing to persist until he had a life-changing breakthrough in that place. He had to see change before he could cross the river!

Don't Tell God What to Do

God won't "deal with us" until we go where He tells us to go. Don't even try to dictate terms to God! God told Jeremiah to get up early and go to the potter's house and He would speak with him there. God will also speak to you exactly where *He chooses.* He is God—and we can't tell Him how or where to talk to us. We cannot manipulate Him either, although many people try to. They act like they can hand Him their resumé and dictate the terms of their "makeover." Don't act as your own advocate and judge; don't tell God what to do.

Jacob obeyed God and went to the place God said He would deal with him. Then Jacob reminded God of His promises:

I am not worthy of the least of all the mercies, and of all the truth, which Thou hast shewed unto Thy servant; for with my staff I passed over this Jordan; and now I am become two bands. Deliver me, I pray Thee, from the hand of my brother, from the hand of Esau: for I fear him, lest he will come and smite me, and the mother with the children. And Thou saidst, I will surely do thee good, and make thy seed as the sand of the sea, which cannot be numbered for multitude (Genesis 32:10-12).

Jacob thought some great blessing was going to occur, but when he got to the Jabbok, he discovered he would have to deal with his past before he could cross. When he reached the bank of the river, his scouts brought him terrifying news: his brother Esau (the brother whose birthright Jacob had stolen!) was advancing to meet him with 400 men (see Gen. 32:6)!

Empty Out the Past

Jacob thought God would "wave a magic wand" and make the past disappear. He was expecting God to make everything easy—wasn't that what He meant when He promised to "do him good"? When he came to the Jabbok River, the threshold of promised fruitfulness and increase, he discovered to his dismay that the past had to be emptied out first...

Have you come to that place? Did you ask God to "deal with you" and "do a good thing," only to have past mistakes and problems suddenly surface? Do you fear that your past will stop or destroy you? Jacob planned for the worst, and split up his family and sent them on across the river, but God let him know that he couldn't follow them. Do you feel like you've done all the work, and all the praying, yet it seems like everyone else just goes on without you? Take heart. God has a plan and purpose—you can trust Him. You will see breakthroughs if you will be persistent like Jacob!

"And Jacob was left alone; and there wrestled a man with him until the breaking of the day" (Gen. 32:24). Is God waiting to get *you alone*? You too will face a struggle before you can cross the river into the promised place of fruitfulness! The struggle will make you *change*. Perhaps you have come to a place where God has dealt with you, but you took it as a negative, and now you think God doesn't care about you. Maybe this place of dealing is a delay or a failure—but if biblical patterns mean anything (and they do!), then God has brought you to a place of struggle *to teach you to persevere*!

Struggles Are Not Failures

Don't grieve God by mistaking your struggles as failures. Don't allow past frustrations and mistakes to hinder the work of the Holy Ghost in your life. God wanted Jacob alone so He could bring him to the point where he was tired of being defeated, frustrated, and afraid! Jacob's lifelong manipulative ways had made his brother, Esau, become his mortal enemy.

Jacob had a good reason to be afraid, and it was rooted in his old identity as a "supplanter and cheat." When he cried out to God, God helped him by bringing him to the point where he was willing to be *changed* and *converted*

to God's way of doing things.
tired, until he was willing to s
God—only bless me." Jacob wen.
He endured the fiery trial that is .
ened faith, and he did not give up or .

Many of us are at the brink of brea.
haven't come to the point of total surrende.   won't
trust God and say, "God, I want what You w   We are
still wrestling with the man, with the flesh, with our own
plans. As you are wrestling, be on guard—don't give up.
The Bible says Jacob and the "man" wrestled until the
breaking of day (see Gen. 32:24). Child of God, *don't give
up now*! *Wrestle until you see daylight.* Wrestle until you
see your change coming! Wrestle until your walk is no
longer the same, and people start noticing that you are
filled with new joy and peace.

Trust Him Anyway!

You may have been at the Jabbok River, on the threshold of blessing and future fruitfulness, for five years! Is
there some "give up" in you right now? Are you thinking,
How am I going to do and be what God wants? Are you
saying, "Nobody loves me. The problems and obstacles
are too great"? God has a way of getting us to the point
where, though it seems impossible, we will decide to
trust Him anyway! A bow and an arrow are powerless
until the string is notched and pulled back first! Sometimes you have to feel like you're backing up before you
can *go forward*!

Don't insult God by wringing your hands and moan-
ing, "Oh God, what am I going to do?" when He sends a
situation or a problem to test you. He is bringing you to

...where you will lift up your head and declare, "...going through. I won't let any past problem, failure, or ruined relationship stop my progress. I'll trust His plan for me!"

Even if your best friend has hurt you, or a devoted friend has left you devastated, God has a plan to help you stand. If you trusted someone in the church with all the private details of your life and they betrayed you, and now you are unwilling to trust again—God wants you to lift your head and trust Him to "do good for you." Do you know that even in times like this, you can declare, "There must be some good in this bad. I will believe that God is going to work all things together for my good!"

Let God's Helpers Help

You may be thinking, "I am not letting anyone close to me ever again! I refuse to open myself to hurt again. I'm not listening to anyone but God." Remember that God sent a "man." Granted, this man was probably supernatural, perhaps even Jesus Himself. The point is that God has a man (or woman) to help you. Even though you're in a hurry, God is still pursuing you. He will continue to bring you to the place where you will persist; where you will view life's trials as opportunities for growth; where you will allow the people He sends to you to help you.

Just as it was in David's life, God intends for the "bear" in your life to prepare you for the "lion" in your life. The "lion" will then prepare you for the "Goliath" in your life (see 1 Sam. 17:34-37). Are you still frustrated and tired of fighting? Have you refused to trust God in your battles? If you have, then you are not willing to go on. You are still viewing trouble in the wrong way.

Are you thinking or saying things like, "Nothing ever works out for me! It seems like everybody else has everything they need, but I'm doing without. My car is always breaking down, but my neighbor's car is too new to break down. I'm serving God, I pray in tongues, and I try hard; but it doesn't look like God is doing anything for me"? It is time to be changed.

God may send brothers and sisters to help you cross the river and get you healed and free of your past. They won't be able to help you if you won't let them get close. Your mind must be renewed and transformed, or you will tell your God-sent messengers, "You're lying to me. There is no promised land. There's no blessing. If God wants to talk person-to-person with me, I'll listen; but I'm not listening to you!"

Stinkin' Thinkin' Stinks

This kind of "stinkin' thinkin' " will produce years or even decades of delay needlessly! God wants to show you how to keep on loving others and blessing them, even past the hurts and disappointments of life. He wants you to learn how to say, "I forgive you, brother, because I want to be like Jesus." Don't flunk "Hurts 101" instead! God wants to bring you to maturity and healing so you can forgive and walk in love, and be free to move onward and upward in God.

God will comfort us and bring us through, if we will trust Him. The day will come when you will be able to embrace those who have broken your heart, for God can put you together again! God is a healer! You can love, even with a broken heart. Love doesn't hurt; only the things we go through hurt. Some of us have flunked our "wrestling class," and we want to quit, but we need to let Him begin to heal those hurts and wounds! We need to enroll again.

Jesus is still asking the same question posed on the first page of this book, "Wilt thou be made whole?" Our prayer is that you will answer with joy, "Sign me up! I'm going to pass this time! I know that the failures and frustrations of my past are not too big for the Greater One who is in me, and who cares so much for me!" It is time for the hurts to meet the Balm of Gilead. This is the day for your deep and hidden wounds to feel the healing touch of your Great Physician, who will only "do good" to you!

End Note

1. *Strong's Concordance*, definition #2999, *yabboq*, derived from #1238, *baqaq* (Hebrew).

A Brief History of the Panama City Fellowship Church of Praise

Fellowship Church of Praise is a balanced, dynamic, and growing ministry located in Panama City, Florida. The first meetings were held at the authors' home in 1974, at Tyndall Air Force Base, beginning with four people who wanted to "learn more about God." By May 1987, they were incorporated as Panama City Fellowship Church of Praise, Inc. The first Church of Praise meeting was held at Laguna Beach Retreat in Panama City Beach with approximately 40 members, and it quickly expanded to a rented church building, which they now own. By May 1991, the first building was paid for and a larger facility purchased. The Lord then told them, "You will build the next one from the ground."

David and Vernette Rosier were ordained with Christian International Network of Prophetic Ministries on February 8, 1989. They each received doctoral degrees from Gulf Coast Seminary on April 19, 1990. In addition to the work in Panama City, they oversee ministries in Tuskegee, Alabama; Macon, Georgia; Marianna, Florida; Daytona Beach, Florida; Port St. Joe, Florida; and Geneva, Switzerland. They also provide oversight to the ministries of several pastors and prophets ordained through Fellowship Church of Praise. David and Vernette are gifted in prophetic ministry, and are recognized for their powerful marriage encounter seminars and leadership training. Their ministry demonstrates a unique blending of spiritual gifts and a unified flow of the Holy Spirit's anointing.

The Rosiers have a mandate from God, a *call to the nations*, to help other churches implement biblical growth principles and broaden their understanding of order in church government and structure. They have raised up qualified associate ministers and elders to help carry the load of this vision, and their motto is: "We Can Do You Good!" (And that's a fact—they do!)

EQUALLY YOKED

by Drs. David and Vernette Rosier.
As we enter the twenty-first century, we will see some ministries become "Elijah" churches. They desire to be on the cutting edge of God's next move, and they endeavor to restore God's glory, power, and anointing to the Church by obtaining proper balance. Equally Yoked shows the need to turn away from the world's system in order to become an Elijah church.
TPB-112p.
ISBN 1-56043-763-4
Retail $7.99

Available at your local Christian bookstore
or by calling Destiny Image toll free:
1-800-722-6774

See all our exciting books on the Internet!
http://www.reapernet.com

The Anointing
Foundation
Facing Yourself
Leadership
Importance of the Arts
Marriage
Team Ministry
Prayer
Gift of Spirit Series

*Please write or phone for a
complete tape list. Your
donations for tapes will be
used to further the work of
the ministry.

Drs. David and Vernette Rosier
2511 E. 3rd St.
Panama City, FL 32401

(904) 769-5442

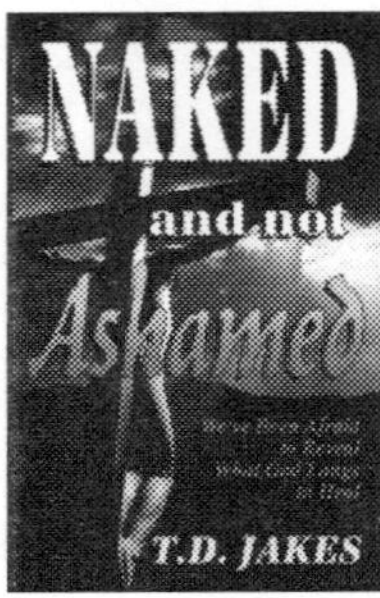

NAKED AND NOT ASHAMED

by T.D. Jakes.

With a powerful anointing, Bishop T.D. Jakes challenges us to go below the surface and become completely and honestly vulnerable before God and man. In relationships, in prayer, in ministry—we need to be willing to be open and transparent. Why do we fear? God already knows us, but He cannot heal our hidden hurts unless we expose them to Him. Only then can we be *Naked and Not Ashamed*!

TPB-156p. ISBN 1-56043-835-5 (6" X 9")
Retail $11.99

CAN YOU STAND TO BE BLESSED?

by T.D. Jakes.

You ask God to bless you and difficulties arise. Why? This book will release the hidden strength within you to go on in God, fulfilling the destiny He has for you. The way to this success is full of twists and turns, yet you can make it through to incredible blessing in your life. The only question left will be, *Can You Stand to Be Blessed?*

TPB-196p. ISBN 1-56043-801-0
Retail $9.99

WOMAN, THOU ART LOOSED!

by T.D. Jakes.

This book offers healing to hurting single mothers, insecure women, and battered wives; and hope to abused girls and women in crisis! Hurting women around the nation—and those who minister to them—are devouring the compassionate truths in Bishop T.D. Jakes' *Woman, Thou Art Loosed!*

TPB-210p. ISBN 1-56043-100-8
Retail $9.99

Available at your local Christian bookstore or by calling Destiny Image toll free:
1-800-722-6774

See all our exciting books on the Internet!
http://www.reapernet.com